The Ward Method

Music Instruction for Catholic Schools

by Justine Ward

STUDENT WORKBOOK I

for use with

THAT ALL MAY SING

Revised Edition 1976

Containing written exercises in:

Intonation

Rhythm

Notation

Creative Activity

Prepared by Theodore Marier

That All May Sing ©1976 by the
Dom Mocquereau Foundation, New York, N.Y.

Student Workbook I for use with *That All May Sing* ©1987 by the
Dom Mocquereau Foundation, New York, N.Y.

Distributed by

Catholic University of America Press
Washington, D.C.

Intonation

Exercise 1   Identify the tones given below by singing each with its proper name:

1 = DO
2 = RE

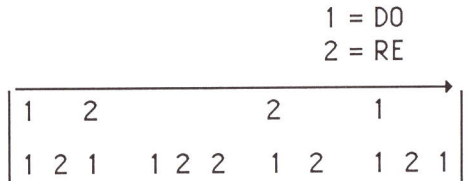

Exercise 2

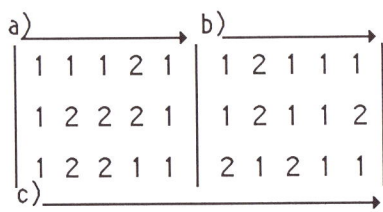

Ear Tests

Rhythm

Rhythm Patterns - **Series 1**   Copy each pattern in the space provided. Sing each one with **Metrical Language** and **Metrical Gesture I**.

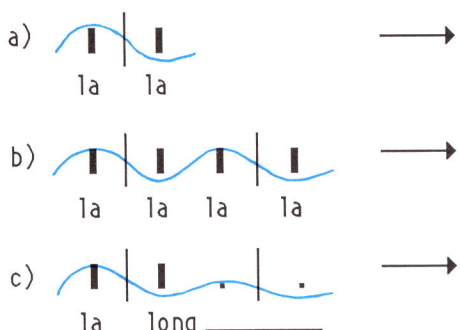

a)   la   la

b)   la   la   la   la

c)   la   long _____

Rhythmic Dictations

Transcription: Place the proper notation number beneath each pitch given.

DO   RE   RE   DO   DO   DO   RE   DO   RE   RE   DO   RE   RE   RE   DO   DO   DO

Sing the series of notes that you have written.

Creative Activity

Compose a melody for the following rhythm pattern.
Use only the tones DO and RE.

Copy each song in the space provided.
Practice each with
- **Metrical Language** and **Metrical Gesture I**
- singing **Note Names** and **Rhythm Gesture** (Wave).

Songs

Song 1

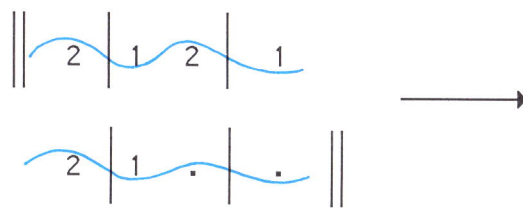

Song 2

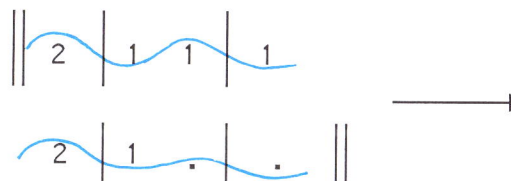

Lesson

Intonation

Exercise 3   Identify tones given below by singing each with its proper name:

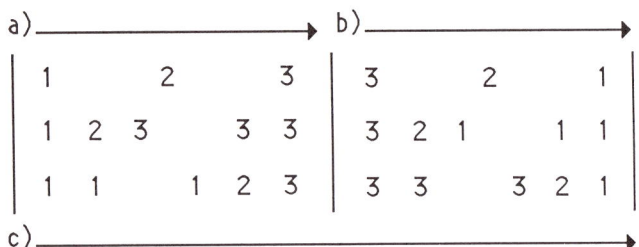

Ear Tests

Rhythm

Review: Rhythm Patterns - **Series 1**

Copy each pattern in the space provided.
Say each while making **Metrical Gesture I**.

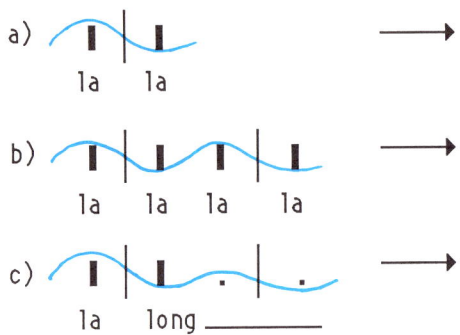

a)   la   la   ⟶

b)   la   la   la   la   ⟶

c)   la   long _____   ⟶

Rhythmic Dictations

Transcription: Place beneath each pitch its proper notation number.

DO   RE   MI   RE   DO   RE   MI   RE   DO

Sing the notes you have written, while making the **Metrical Gesture**.

Creative Activity

Compose a melody for the following rhythm pattern.
Use only the tones studied thus far:

1 = DO 2 = RE 3 = MI

Songs

Copy each song in the space provided.
Practice singing each with **Note Names** and **Metrical Gesture I**;
then sing each with **Note Names** and **Rhythm Gesture** (Wave).

Song 3
 b)
 c)
 b)
 c)

Song 4
 b)
 c)
 b)
 c)

Song 5

Song 6

Words and Melody

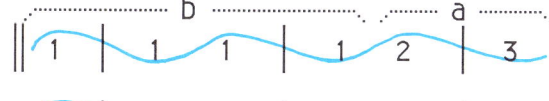

A- men._____

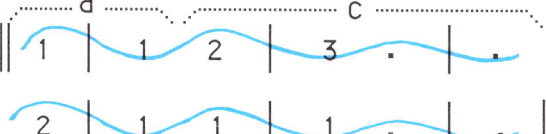

A- men._____

Al- le- lu- ia._____

Lesson 3   Vocal Training

Intonation

Identify each pitch with its correct name as you sing each line. The dot (.) tells you to hum softly the note you have just sung. Later, the dot (.) will tell you to "think" the same note and not sing it.

Exercise 4   Introduces the think tones.

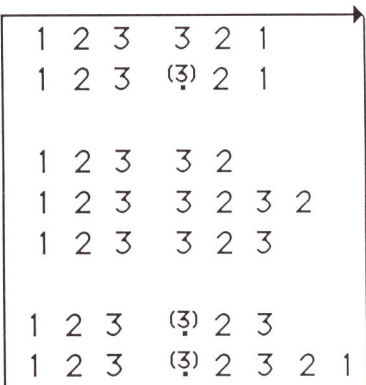

```
1  2  3    3  2  1
1  2  3   (3) 2  1

1  2  3    3  2
1  2  3    3  2  3  2
1  2  3    3  2  3

1  2  3   (3) 2  3
1  2  3   (3) 2  3  2  1
```

Exercise 5

This exercise adds two more tones to the scale line: 4 = FA

5 = SOL

a) ──────────→ b) ──────────────→

```
| 1 2 3 4 5       | 5 4 3 2 1       |
| 1 2 3 4 5 5 5   | 5 4 3 2 1 1 1   |
| 1 1 1 2 3 4 5   | 5 5 5 4 3 2 1   |
```

c) ──────────────────────────→

Ear Tests

Rhythm   Rhythm Patterns - **Series 2**   Melodic Application

a)

b)

New c)

New d)

```
2 | 1 | 2 | 3

2 | 1 . | .

1 | 1 2 | 3 3 | 3

3 | 3 2 | 1 . | .
```

Creative Activity

Compose a melody for the rhythm given:

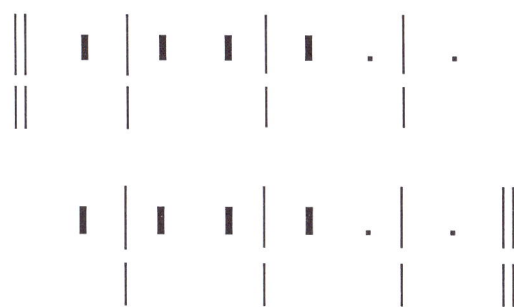

Transcription: Place the proper notation number beneath each pitch.

DO   RE   MI   FA   FA   SOL   SOL   SOL   SOL   FA   FA   MI   FA   MI   RE   DO

Sing the entire series of notes while making the correct **Measuring Gesture**.

Practice singing with **Note Names** and **Metrical Gesture**.
Repeat with **Rhythm Gesture**.

Songs

Song 7

Song 8

d) ‖ 1 | 1 2 | 3 . | .

d) 2 | 3 2 | 1 . | . ‖

Song 9

a) ‖ 1 | 1 2 | 1

d) 1 | 1 2 | 3 . | .

a) 3 | 3 3 | 3

d) 3 | 3 2 | 1 . | . ‖

Song 10

c) 1 | 1 2 | 3 4 | 5

d) 5 | 5 5 | 5 . | .

c) 5 | 5 4 | 3 2 | 1 ‖

See Page 48 for **THE FLOWERS AWAKE**

Vocal Training

Intonation

Exercise 6

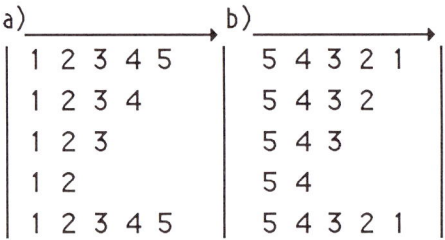

a)						b)					
1	2	3	4	5		5	4	3	2	1	
1	2	3	4			5	4	3	2		
1	2	3				5	4	3			
1	2					5	4				
1	2	3	4	5		5	4	3	2	1	

Exercise 7

a)									b)								
1	2	3	4	5		5	5	5	5	4	3	2	1		1	1	1
1	2	3	4			4	4	4	5	4	3	2			2	2	2
1	2	3				3	3	3	5	4	3				3	3	3
1	2					2	2	2	5	4					4	4	4
1	2	3	4	5	5	4	3	2	1	5	4	3	2	1	1	1	1

Exercise 8

a)									b)								
1	2	3	4	5					5	4	3	2	1				
1	2	3	4				4	5	5	4	3	2				2	1
1	2	3				3	4	5	5	4	3			3	2	1	
1	2				2	3	4	5	5	4			4	3	2	1	

c) ⟶

Ear Tests

Creative Activity

Practice with:
- **Metrical Gesture I**
- **Metrical Language**
- **Rhythm Gesture II**

Rhythm Patterns - **Series 2**   Melodic Application

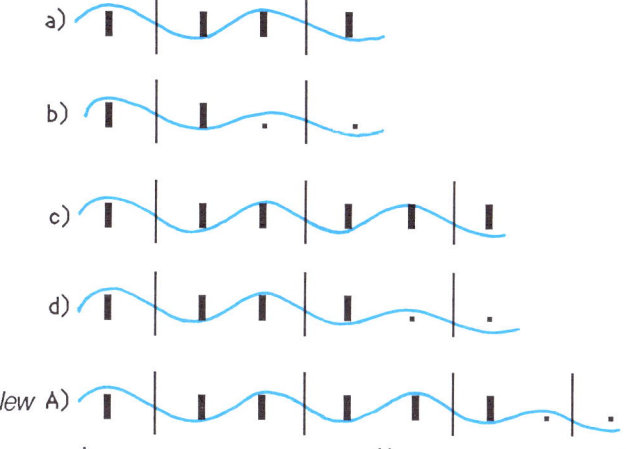

a)   2 | 1   2 | 3

b)   2   1 | . | .

c)   3 | 3   2 | 1   2 | 3

d)   3 | 3   2 | 1   . | .

New A)   2 | 1   2 | 3   2 | 1   . | .

         a   b

Rhythmic Dictations

Songs

Song 11

a) || 1   1 2 | 3

d)   3 | 3 4 | 5 . | .

a)   5 | 5 4 | 3

d)   3 | 3 2 | 1 . | . ||

Song 12

                           a   b

A (a+b) || 1   1 2 | 3 4 | 5 . | .

              5 | 5 5 | 5 5 | 5 . | .

              5 | 5 4 | 3 2 | 1 . | . ||

Song 13

A (a+b) || 1   1 | 2 | 3 4 | 5 . | .

d)   5 | 5 4 | 3 . | .

d)   3 | 3 4 | 5 . | .

A (a+b)   5 | 5 4 | 3 2 | 1 . | . ||

Vocal Training

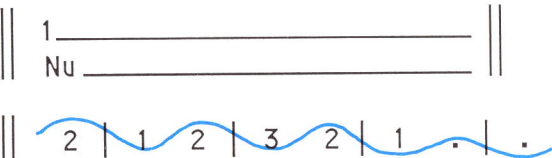

Intonation

Review:

Ex. 9
```
| 1 2 3 4 5 5 5   5 4 3 2 1 1 1 |
| 1 2 3     3 4 5   5 4 3   3 2 1 |
| 1 2 3 3 3 4 5   5 4 3 3 3 2 1 |
```

Ex. 10
```
| 1 2 3 4 5     5 4 3 2 1 |
| 1 2 3 4       4 3 2 1 |
| 1 2 3           3 2 1 |
| 1 2               2 1 |
| 1 2 3 4 5     5 4 3 2 1 |
```

Ex. 11
```
| 1 2 3 4 5     5 4 3 2 1 |
| 1 2 3 4 5   . 4 3 2 1 |
| 1 2 3 4       4 3 2 1 |
| 1 2 3 4     . 3 2 1 |
| 1 2 3         3 2 1 |
| 1 2 3       . 2 1 |
| 1 2           2 1 |
| 1 2         . 1 |
```

Ear Tests

Rhythm

Copy rhythm patterns in the space provided. Add rhythm wave.

a)

b)

c)

Combine rhythms as indicated and compose a melody for each.

a) + c)

b) + c)

Rhythmic Dictations

Notation

Transcribe the numbers to staff.
Sing the notes while making the **Measuring Gesture**.

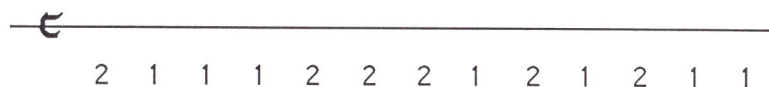

¢   2   1   1   1   2   2   2   1   2   1   2   1   1

Songs

Sing each song first with **Metrical Gesture I**, then with **Rhythm Gesture I**.
Add rhythm wave.

Song 14

(a + c) || 1 | 1 2 | 3 3 | 3 . | .

3 | 3 4 | 5 5 | 5 . | .

5 | 5 4 | 3 3 | 3 . | .

3 | 3 2 | 1 1 | 1 . | . ||

Song 15

(a + b + c) || 2 | 1 1 | 1

2 | 1 . | 1

2 | 1 . | . ||

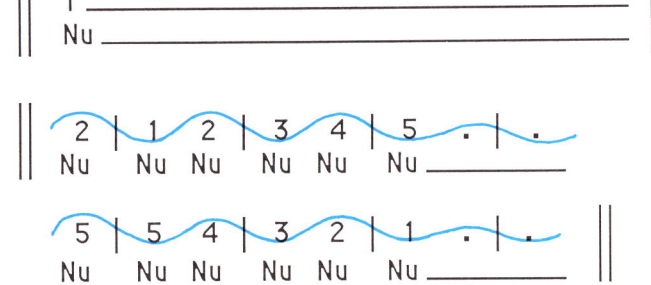

Vocal Training

| 1 | _____ |
| Nu | _____ |

| 2 | 1 | 2 | 3 | 4 | 5 | . | . |
| Nu | Nu | Nu | Nu | Nu | Nu _____ |

| 5 | 5 | 4 | 3 | 2 | 1 | . | . |
| Nu | Nu | Nu | Nu | Nu | Nu _____ |

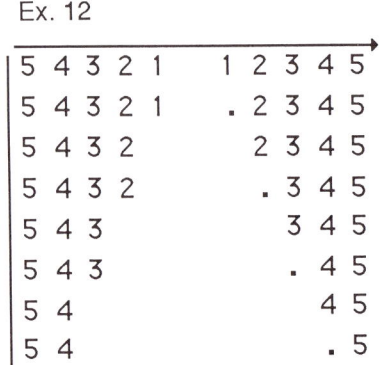

Ex. 12

```
5 4 3 2 1    1 2 3 4 5
5 4 3 2 1    . 2 3 4 5
5 4 3 2        2 3 4 5
5 4 3 2        . 3 4 5
5 4 3            3 4 5
5 4 3            . 4 5
5 4                4 5
5 4                . 5
```

Ex. 13

```
1   2    3    4    5    5    4    3    2    1
12   12        34   5    5 4        54   32   1
12   3 4       34   5    5 4        32   32   1
```

Ex. 14

```
1 2 3 4 5    5 4 3 2 1
1 1 2 1 2    2 1 2 1 1
1 2 1 2 2    1 2 2 2 1
```

Ear Tests

Rhythm

Copy the rhythm patterns in the space provided. Add rhythm wave.

a) ▌ | ▌ | ▌ | ▌

b) ▌ | ▌ | . | ▌

c) ▌ | ▌ | . | .

d) ▌ | ▌ | . | ▌ | . | ▌ | . | .

Combine the following patterns and compose a melody for each.

a) + b)

a) + c)

b) + c)

Notation

Transcribe numbers to staff. Sing the notes from the staff while using the **Measuring Gesture**.

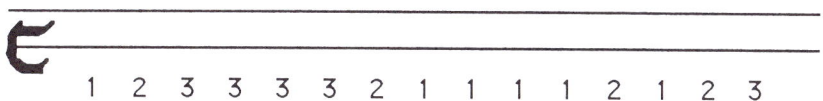

1 2 3 3 3 3 2 1 1 1 1 2 1 2 3

Songs

Song 16

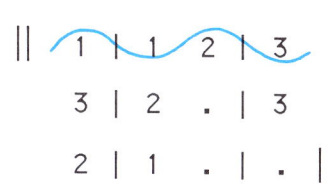

3 | 2 . | 3

2 | 1 . | . ||

Song 17

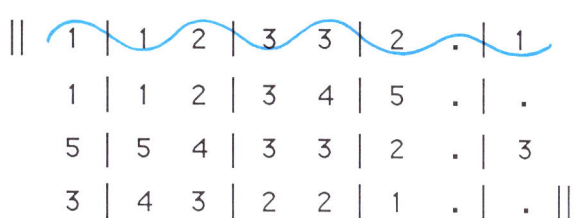

1 | 1 2 | 3 4 | 5 . | .

5 | 5 4 | 3 3 | 2 . | 3

3 | 4 3 | 2 2 | 1 . | . ||

1. Say rhythm with **Metrical Gesture I** and **Metrical Language**.
2. Say note names with **Metrical Gesture I**.
3. Sing note names with **Metrical Gesture I**.

4. Sing note names with **Rhythm Gesture II or III**.
5. Say words in correct rhythm.
6. Sing words with **Rhythm Gesture II or III**.

BEFORE I GO TO SLEEP

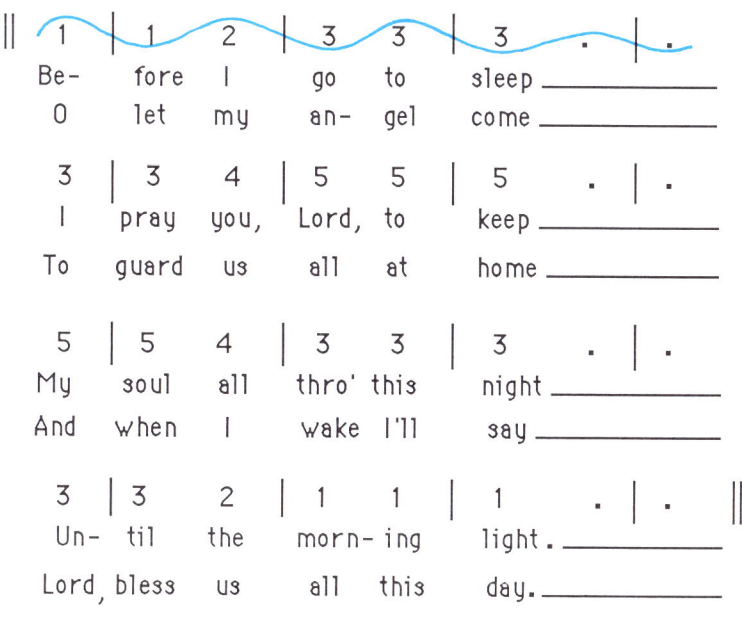

|| 1   1   2 | 3   3 | 3   . | .
  Be- fore I   go   to   sleep _____
  O   let   my   an- gel come _____

3 | 3   4 | 5   5 | 5   . | .
I   pray you, Lord, to keep _____
To guard us   all at   home _____

5 | 5   4 | 3   3 | 3   . | .
My soul all thro' this night _____
And when I   wake I'll say _____

3 | 3   2 | 1   1 | 1   . | . ||
Un- til the morn-ing light. _____
Lord, bless us all this day. _____

Rhythmic Dictations

AMEN || 1   2 . | . ||
          A- men. ____

Lesson **7**

```
|| 1 _____
|| Nu _____ ||
```

Vocal Training

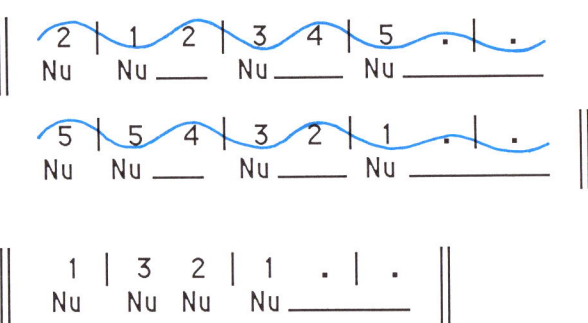

```
|| 2 | 1  2 | 3  4 | 5  .  | .
   Nu   Nu ___  Nu ____  Nu _____
```

```
   5 | 5  4 | 3  2 | 1  .  | .
   Nu   Nu ___  Nu ____  Nu _____  ||
```

```
|| 1 | 3  2 | 1  .  | .  ||
   Nu   Nu Nu   Nu _____
```

Intonation

Ex .15

1	2	3	4	5		5	4	3	2	1
1	2	3	3	2		3	2	1	2	3
3	2	2	3	2		3	2	2	3	3
3	2	3	2	3		3	2	3	2	1

Ear Tests

Ex. 16

a)
1	2	3
1	2	3
1	.	

b)
3	2	1
3	2	1
3	.	

c)
1	2	3		3	2	1
1		3		3		1

Rhythmic Dictations

Rhythm

Copy rhythm patterns in the space provided. Sing on one tone while making **Metrical Gesture I** and using **Metrical Language**.

a)

b)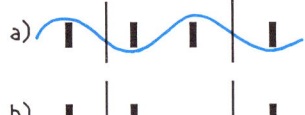

c)

d)

Combine rhythm patterns as indicated. Compose a melody for each.

a) + b)   b) + c)

a) + c)

Notation

Transcriptions

a) Transcribe the numbers given to Staff Notation.

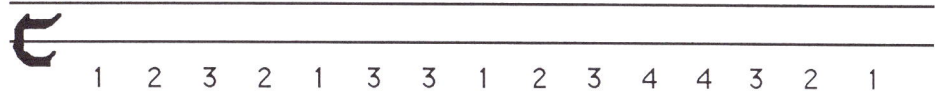

Sing the note names from the staff while using the **Measuring Gesture**.

b) Transcribe the rhythm strokes to corresponding notes in Staff Notation.

Songs

Sing each song with the correct Rhythm Gesture.

N.B.

Song 18   ‖ 3 | 1 2 | 3 2 | 3 . | .
                3 | 1 2 | 3 4 | 5 . | .
                5 | 5 4 | 3 2 | 3 . | .
                2 | 1 3 | 2 2 | 1 . | . ‖

Song 19   ‖ 2 | 1 2 | 3 4 | 3 . | .
                4 | 3 . | 3 . | 2 . | .
                2 | 3 4 | 5 5 | 5 . | .
                5 | 4 3 | 2 2 | 1 . | . ‖

Words and Melody

‖ 5 | 5 4 | 3 . | 3 . | . ‖
Al- le- lu- ia _____

‖ 1 | 2 3 | 1 . | . ‖
Al- le- lu- ia _____

N.B.: Note skip.

Lesson 8

Vocal Training

```
|| 1 _____ ||
   Nu _____

|| 2 | 1  2 | 3  4 | 5  .  | .  ||
   Nu   Nu ___  Nu ___  Nu ___

|| 5 | 5  4 | 3  2 | 1  .  | .  ||
   Nu   Nu ___  Nu ___  Nu ___

|| 1 | 3  2 | 1  .  | .  ||
   Nu   Nu  Nu  Nu ___
```

Intonation

Ex. 17
```
| 1  2  3  4  5      5  5  5      5  6  5      5  4  3  2  1
| 1  2  3  4  5  6  5      5  6  5  6  5  5   5  6  5  4  3  2  1
```
New: 6 = LA

Ex. 18
```
| 1  2  3  4  5  6  5      5  6  6      6  6  5      5  6  5  4  3  2  1
| 1  2  3  4  5  6         6  6  6      6  5  6      5  6  5  4  3  2  1
```

Ex. 19
```
| 1  2  3  4  5      5  4  3  2  1
| 1  2  3  4         4  3
| 1  2  3  4         .  3
| 1  2  3  4         4  3  4  3
| 1  2  3  4         .  3  4  3  2
| 1  2  3  4         .  3  2
| 1  2  3  4         .  3  2  1
```

Ear Tests

Rhythmic Dictations

Rhythm

Think of words that fit the following rhythm patterns:

a) ▮ | ▮ | ▮ | ▮

b) ▮ | ▮ . | ▮

c) ▮ | ▮ . | .

Combine the patterns and compose melodies for each combination.

a) + b) + c)

b) + a) + c)

Notation **Transcriptions**

Transcribe the numbers to Staff Notation.

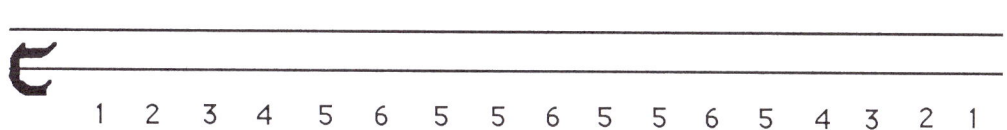

1 2 3 4 5 6 5 5 6 5 5 6 5 4 3 2 1

Transcribe the following rhythm strokes to corresponding staff notes:

Songs

Song 20

|| 1 ⌢ | 1 2 | 3 4 | 5 ⌢ . | .
5 | 5 6 | 5 6 | 5 . | .
5 | 6 . | 5 4 | 3 . | .
2 | 1 . | 2 . | 1 . | . ||

Song 21

|| 1 ⌢ | 1 2 | 3 4 | 5 ⌢ . | .
5 | 6 . | 6 . | 5 . | .
5 | 5 6 | 5 4 | 3 . | .
4 | 3 . | 2 . | 1 . | . ||

WE THANK YOU, GOD, FOR EVERYTHING

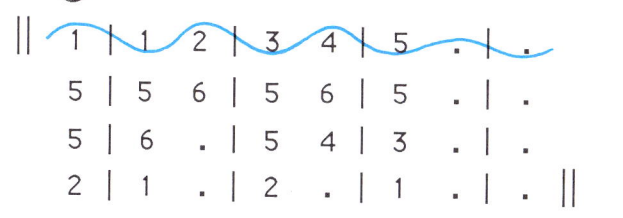

|| 2 ⌢ | 1 1 | 2 | 3 3 | 3 ⌢ . | .
We   thank you,   God, for   flow- ers sweet: _____

4 | 3 3 | 3 4 | 5 5 | 5 . | .
We   thank you   for   the   food we   eat; _____

5 | 5 5 | 5 5 | 6 6 | 5 . | .
We   thank you   for   the   birds that   sing; _____

4 | 5 5 | 5 4 | 3 2 | 1 . | . ||
We   thank you,   God, for   ev -'ry - thing. _____

Lesson 9

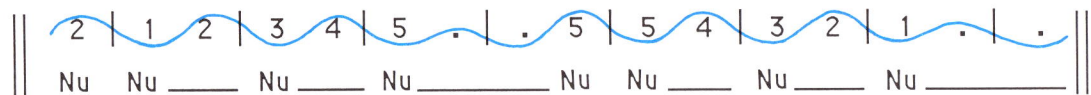

Vocal Training

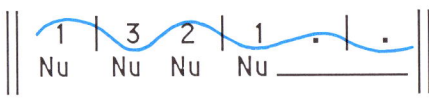

Intonation

Sing with **Measuring Gesture:**

Ex. 20

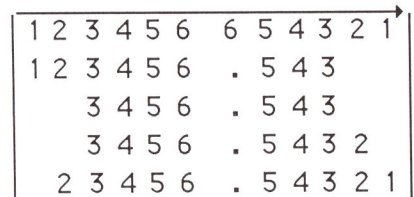

Ex. 21

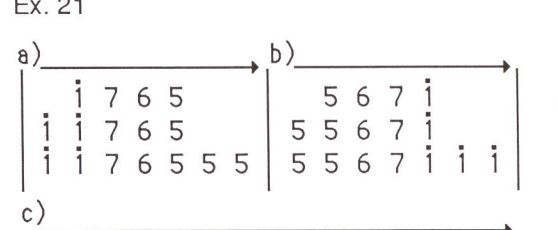

New: 7 = TI

i̇ = high DO

Ear Tests

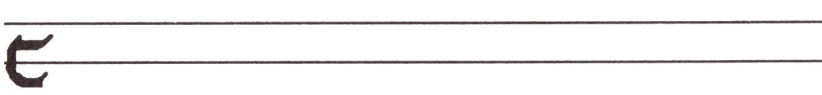

Rhythm

Rhythm Patterns - **Series 5**

Copy the rhythm patterns in the space provided.
New: **Ternary Rhythm**: Three pulses in a full measure.

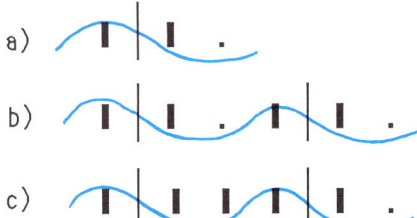

Combine the patterns as indicated and compose a melody for each. Add rhythm wave.

b) + b)

c) + a)

Staff Notation

Transcribe the rhythms given to Staff Notation:

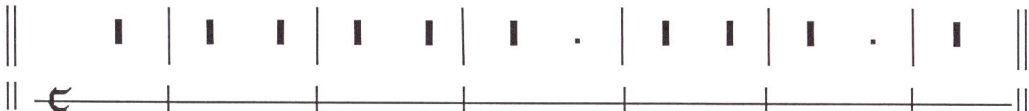

Sing the notes given. Then write the notes on the staff as you sing them again.

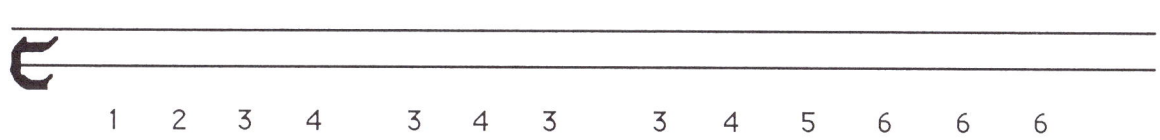

1   2   3   4   3   4   3   3   4   5   6   6   6

Songs

Song 22

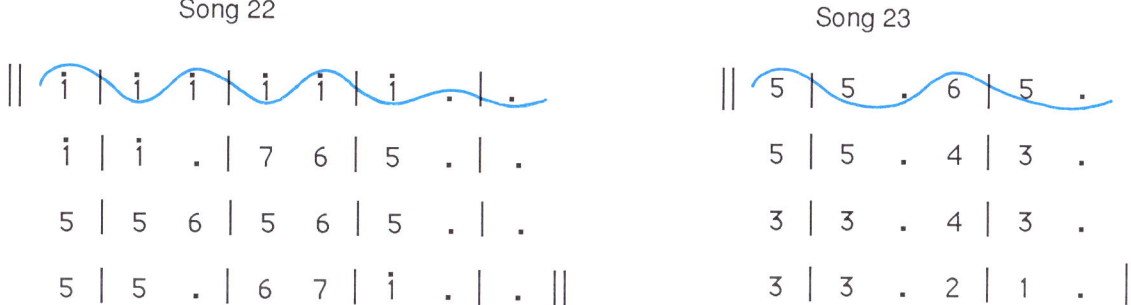

î | î . | 7 6 | 5 . | .

5 | 5 6 | 5 6 | 5 . | .

5 | 5 . | 6 7 | î . | . ‖

Song 23

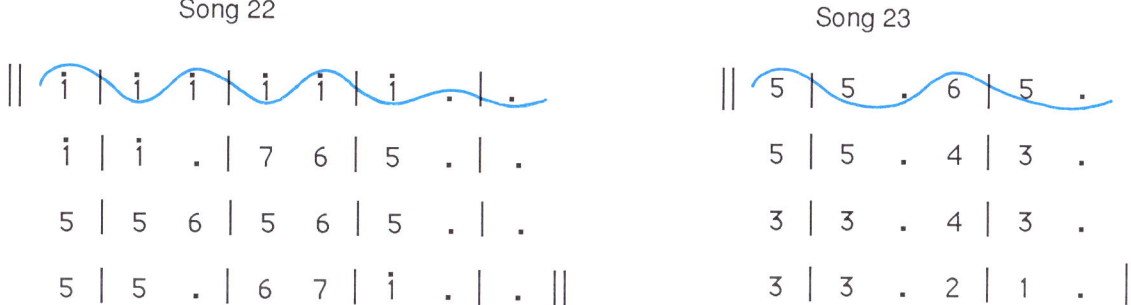

5 | 5 . 4 | 3 .

3 | 3 . 4 | 3 .

3 | 3 . 2 | 1 . ‖

I SAW A SHIP A-SAILING

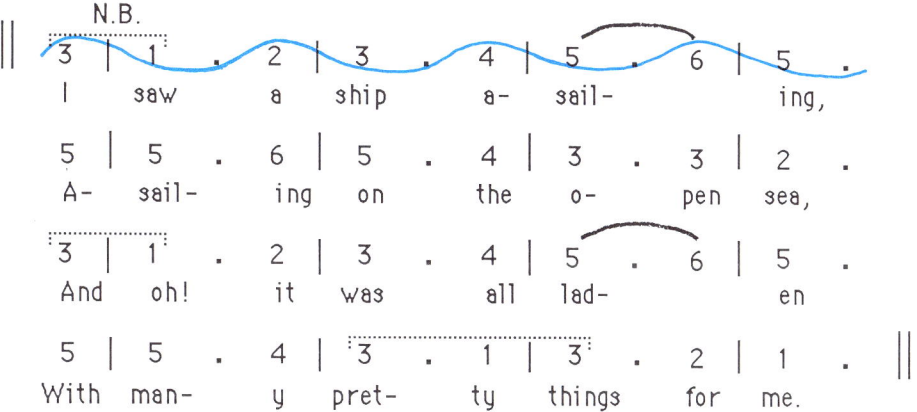

N.B.

‖ 3 | 1 . 2 | 3 . 4 | 5 . 6 | 5 .
  I   saw   a   ship   a-   sail-   ing,

5 | 5 . 6 | 5 . 4 | 3 . 3 | 2 .
A-   sail-   ing   on   the   o-   pen   sea,

3 | 1 . 2 | 3 . 4 | 5 . 6 | 5 .
And   oh!   it   was   all   lad-   en

5 | 5 . 4 | 3 . 1 | 3 . 2 | 1 . ‖
With   man-   y   pret-   ty   things   for   me.

N.B.: Note Skip. See exercise 16 on page 14.

Lesson 10

Vocal Training

‖ 1 _____ ‖
Nu _____

‖ 2 | 1 2 | 3 4 | 5 . | . 5 | 5 4 | 3 2 | 1 . | . ‖
Nu   Nu __ Nu __ Nu __ Nu Nu __ Nu __ Nu __

‖ 1 | 3 2 | 1 . | . ‖   ‖ i̅ | 7 6 | 5 . | . ‖
Nu Nu Nu Nu _____   Nu Nu Nu Nu _____

Intonation

Ex. 22

a) →
| i̅ 7 6 5 |
| i̅ 7 6 |
| i̅ 7 |
| i̅ 7 6 5 |

b) →
| 5 6 7 i̅ |
| 5 6 7 |
| 5 6 |
| 5 6 7 i̅ |

Ex. 23

a) →
| i̅ 7 6 5   5 5 5 |
| i̅ 7 6   6 6 6 |
| i̅ 7   7 7 7 |
| i̅ 7 6 5   5 5 5 |

b) →
| 5 6 7 i̅   i̅ i̅ i̅ |
| 5 6 7   7 7 7 |
| 5 6   6 6 6 |
| 5 6 7 i̅   i̅ i̅ i̅ |

Ex. 24 →

| i̅ 7 6 5   5 5 5   5 6 7 i̅   i̅ i̅ i̅ |
| i̅ 7 6   6 6 5   5 6 6   6 7 i̅ |
| i̅ 7   7 6 5   5 6   6 7 i̅ |
| i̅ 7 6 5   5 6 7 i̅ |

Ex. 25 →

| i̅ 7 6 5   5 4 3   3 4 5   5 6 7 i̅ |

Ear Tests

Rhythmic Dictations

Rhythm

Copy each rhythm pattern in the space provided and add the rhythm wave for each.

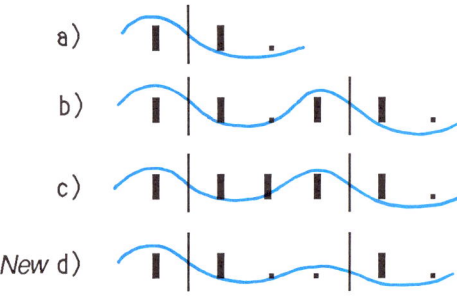

a)

b)

c)

New d)

Rhythm (Continued) Combine patterns as indicated. Compose a melody for each.

b) + c)

c) + d)

Notation

1. Transcribe the Rhythm Strokes to Staff Notation in the following.
2. Sing with **Metrical Gesture I** and **Metrical Language**.

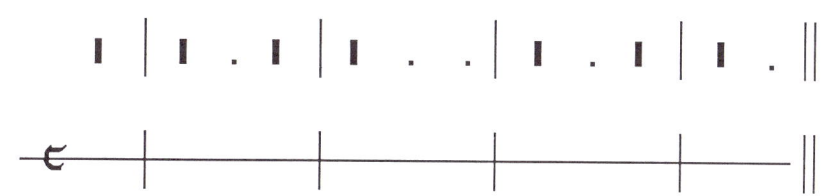

Time values of notes in Staff Notation:

3. Transcribe the following melody to Staff Notation.
4. Sing on note names while making **Rhythm Gesture III**.

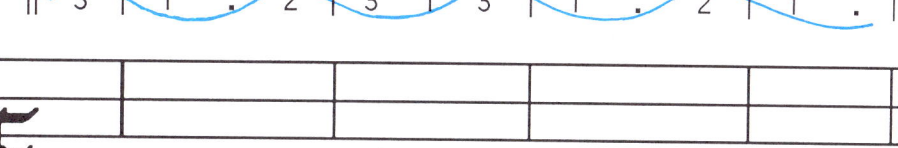

Songs

Song 24

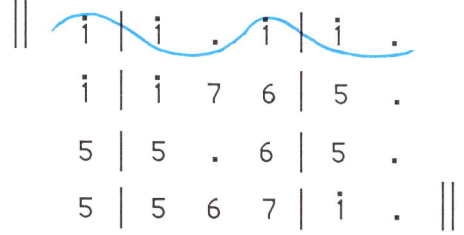

Song 25

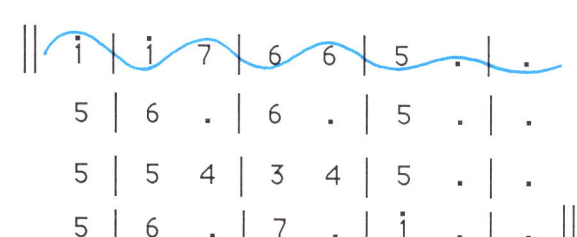

O COME, O COME, EMMANUEL

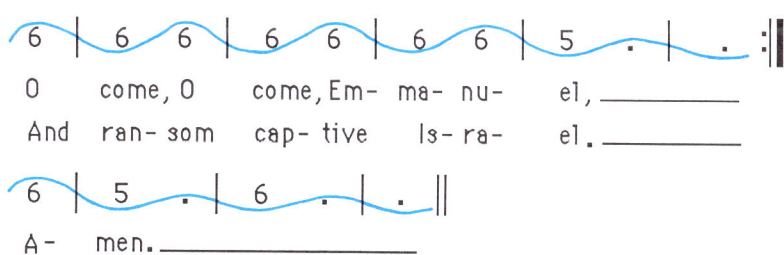

O come, O come, Em-ma-nu-el,_____
And ran-som cap-tive Is-ra-el._____

A-men._____

Lesson 11

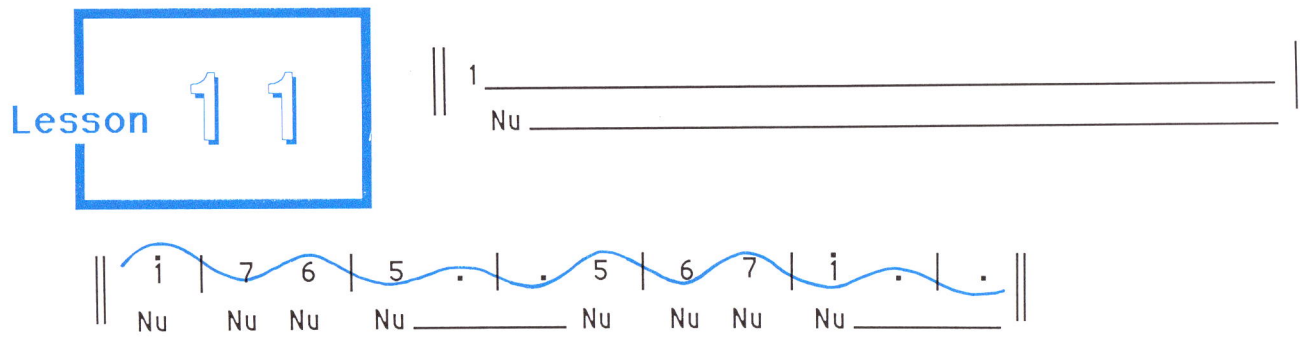

Intonation

Sing each line while making the **Measuring Gesture**.

Ex. 26

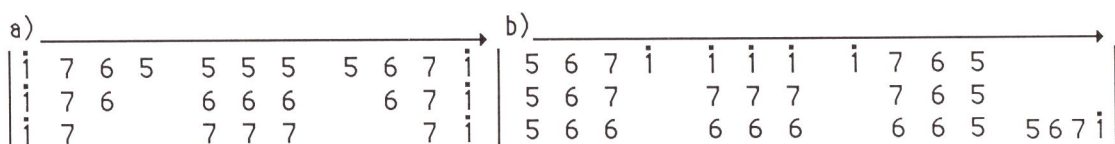

a)											
í	7	6	5	5	5	5	5	6	7	í	
í	7	6		6	6	6		6	7	í	
í	7			7	7	7			7	í	

b)											
5	6	7	í	í	í	í	í	7	6	5	
5	6	7		7	7	7		7	6	5	
5	6	6		6	6	6		6	6	5	5 6 7 í

Ex. 27

í	7	6	5	5	6	7	í
í	7	6	5	.	6	7	í
í	7	6			6	7	í
í	7	6			.	7	í
í	7					7	í
í	7					.	í

Ear Tests

Notation

Transcribe the following notes to Staff Notation:

í í 7 6 5 5 5 5   5 6 7 í í í

Sing the notes as you write them.

Rhythm

Study each pattern as follows:
1. Say rhythm with **Metrical Gesture I** and **Metrical Language**.
2. Say note-names with **Metrical Gesture**.
3. Sing note-names with **Metrical Gesture**.
4. Sing note-names with **Rhythm Gesture III**.

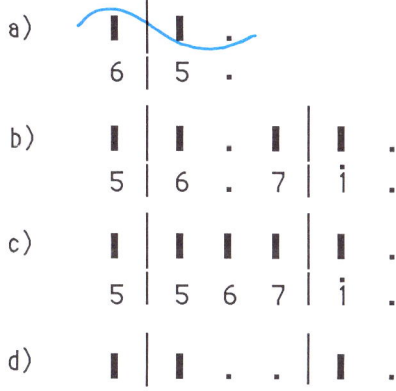

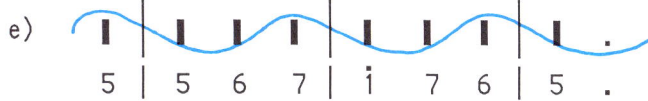

Draw the correct rhythm wave for each pattern

Rhythmic Dictations

Songs

Study each song according the the directions given for studying the rhythms above.

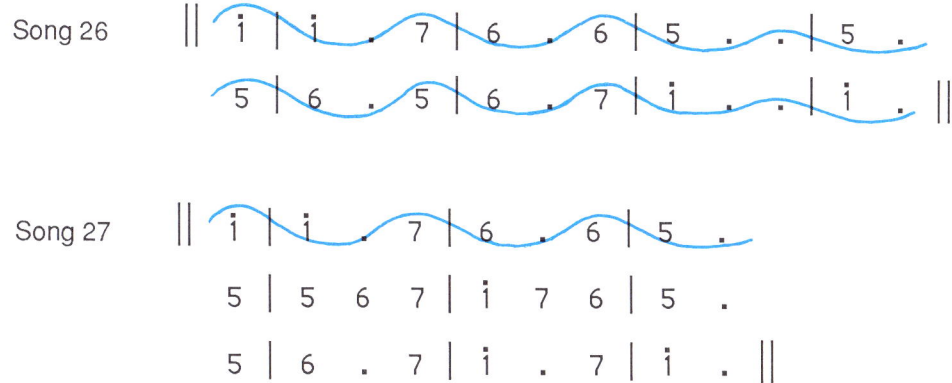

Song 26

Song 27

5 | 5 6 7 | i̇ 7 6 | 5 .

5 | 6 . 7 | i̇ . 7 | i̇ . ‖

See Page 48 for **REJOICE, REJOICE, O ISRAEL**

Lesson **12**

Intonation

EX. 28

```
1 7 6 5    5 6 5   5 6 7 1   7 1
1 7 6 5    6 6     6 5 6 7   1 1
1 7 6 7    6 6     6 7 6 7   1 1
1 7 6 5    6 5     5 6 7 1   7 1
```

EX. 29

```
1 7   1 7 6   5 6 5 6 5
6 5   6 5 6   6 5 6 7 1
1 7   6 6 5   5 6 6 5 6
6 5   6 6 5   6 7 1 7 1
```

EX. 30

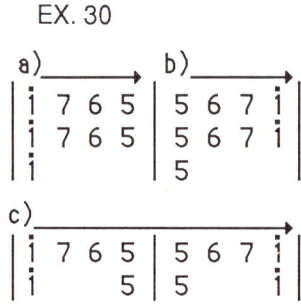

a)
```
1 7 6 5
1 7 6 5
1
```
b)
```
5 6 7 1
5 6 7 1
5
```

c)
```
1 7 6 5 | 5 6 7 1
1     5 | 5     1
```

Ear Tests

Notation

Transcribe Song 31.
Add rhythm wave to numbers and sing.

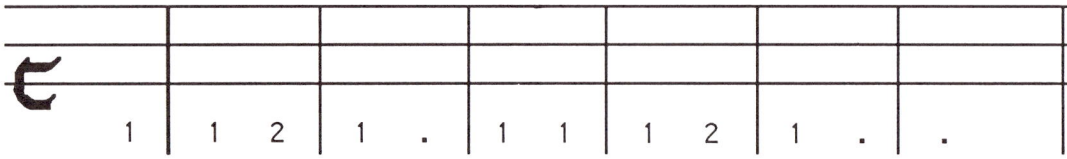

```
1 | 1 2 | 1 . | 1 1 | 1 2 | 1 . | .
```

Rhythm

Draw the rhythm wave for each pattern.
Compose a melody for each.

e)

A)

f)

Rhythmic Dictations

Songs

Study each song as follows:

1. Say rhythm with **Metrical Gesture I** and **Metrical Language**.
2. Say note-names with **Metrical Gesture I**.
3. Sing note-names with **Metrical Gesture I**.
4. Sing note-names with **Rhythm Gesture II or III**.
5. Sing words in correct rhythm.
6. Sing words with **Rhythm Gesture II or III**.

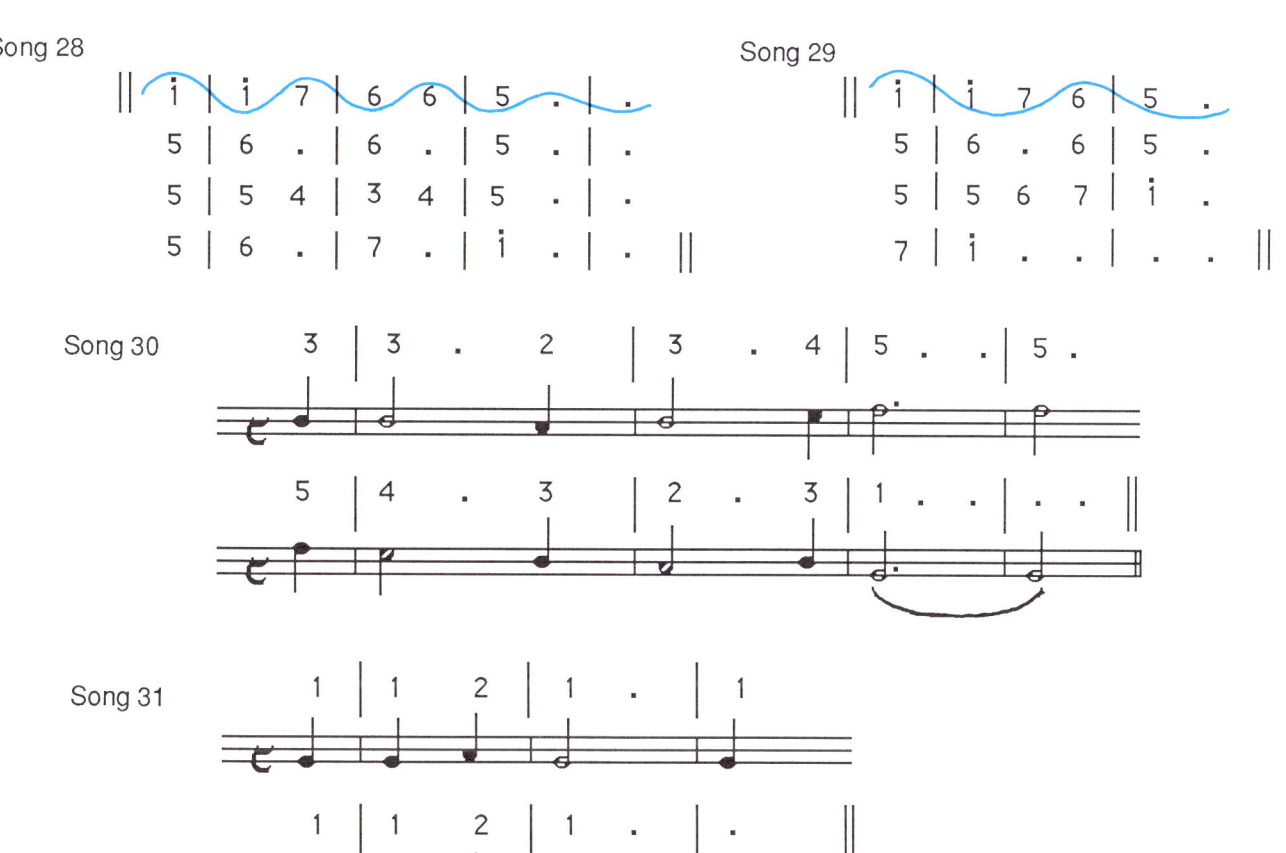

Song 28

Song 29

Song 30

Song 31

See Page 48 for
A CHILD IS BORN IN BETHLEHEM

Lesson 13

Intonation

Vocal Training

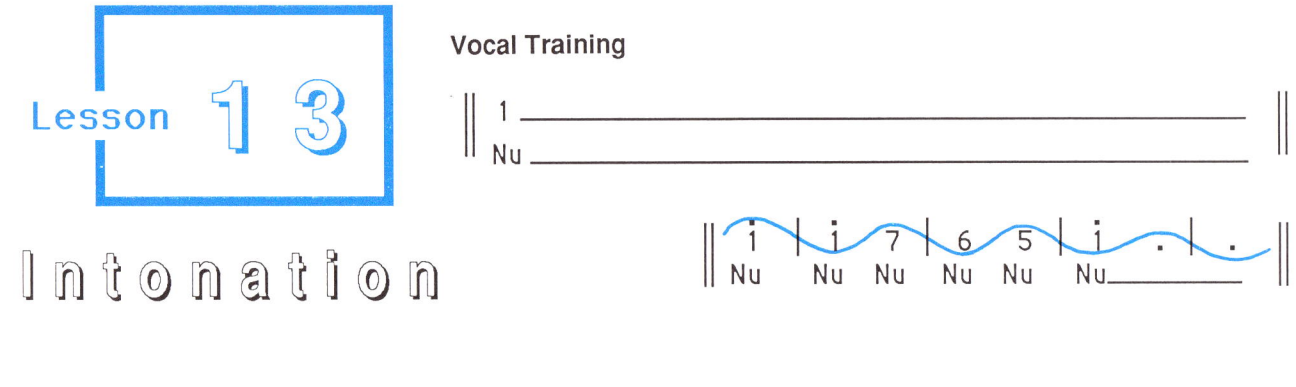

Ex. 31

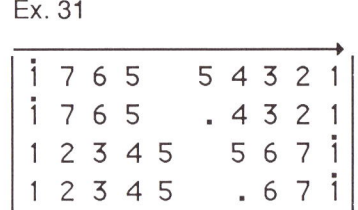

Ex. 32

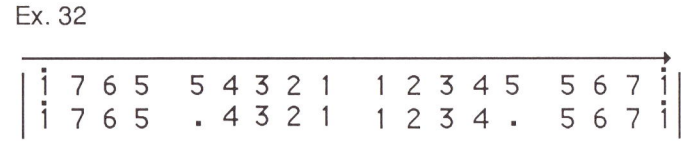

Ear and Eye Tests

Rhythm

Study each pattern with **Rhythm Gesture I** and **Metrical Language**.
Draw the rhythm wave for each pattern.
Compose a melody for each pattern.

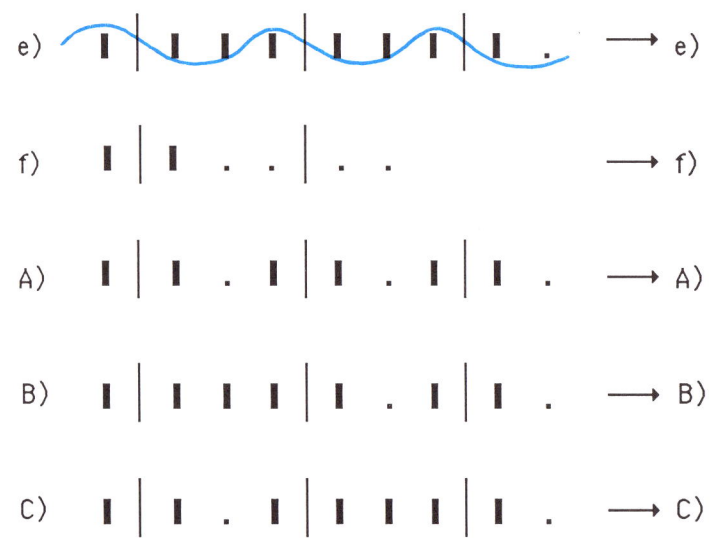

e) ⟶ e)

f) ⟶ f)

A) ⟶ A)

B) ⟶ B)

C) ⟶ C)

Rhythmic Dictations

N o t a t i o n

Transcribe each of the examples given.

1. From Staff Notation to Number Notation.

2. From Number Notation to Staff Notation.

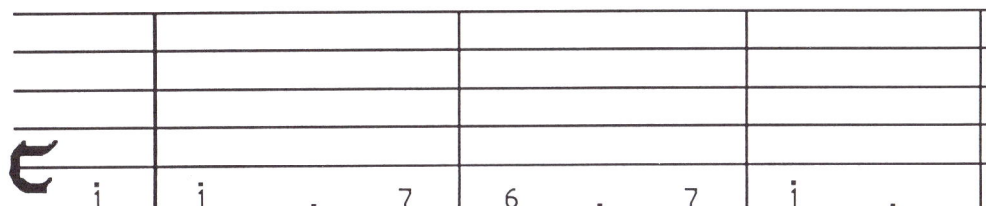

C r e a t i v e   A c t i v i t y

Compose a two line melody
for the rhythm patterns given.

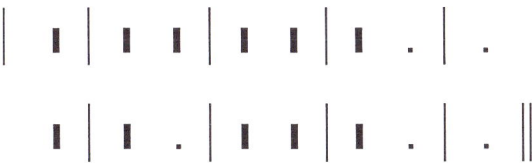

S o n g s

Song 32

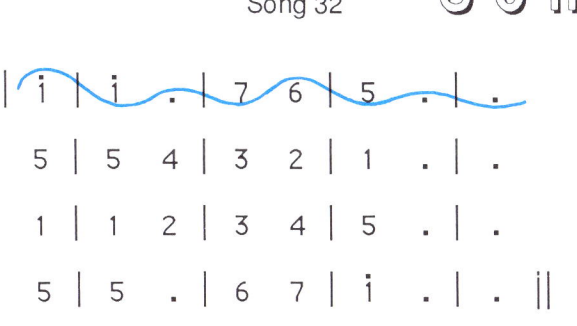

Song 33

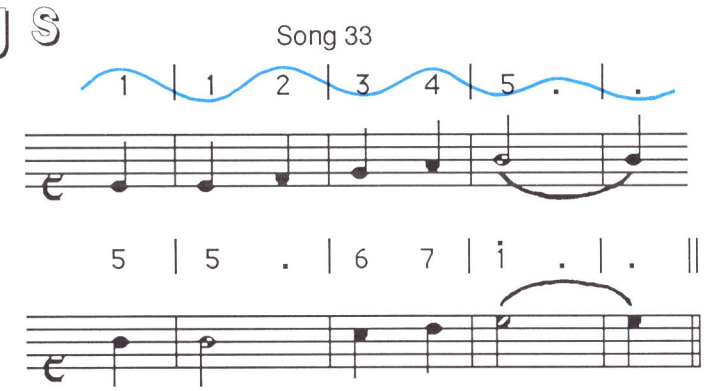

IF ALL THE WORLD WERE PAPER

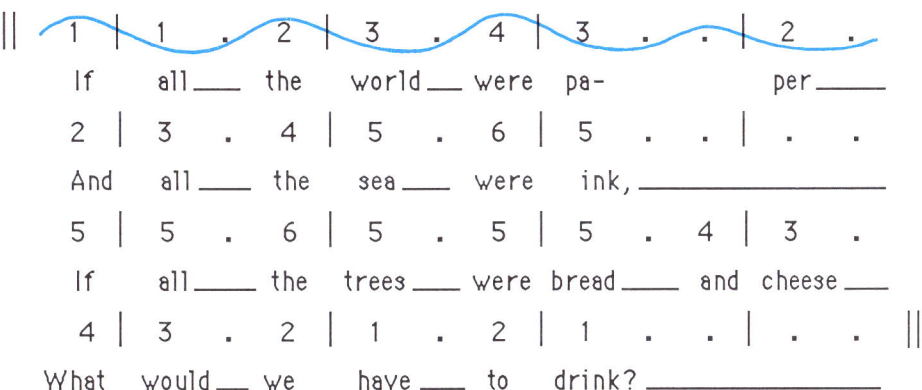

Intonation

Vocal Training

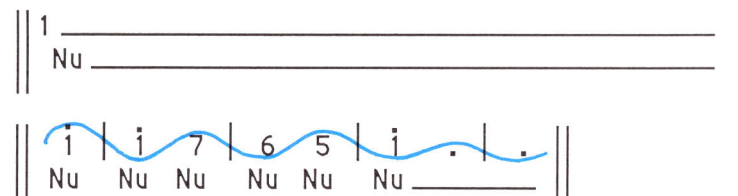

Ex. 33 - The Family of DO

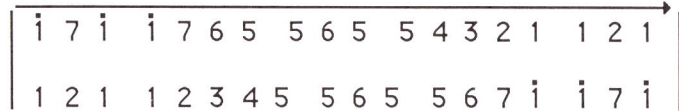

Staff Notation

Ear and Eye Tests

Rhythm

Study the following rhythms.
Draw the correct rhythm waves for each.
Compose a melody for each.

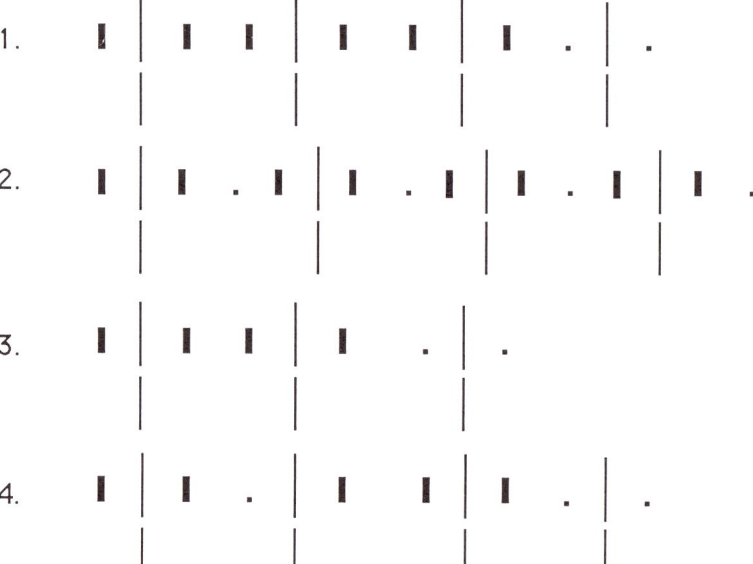

Rhythmic Dictations

Staff Notation Transcribe each of the examples given:

1. From Number Notation to Staff Notation.

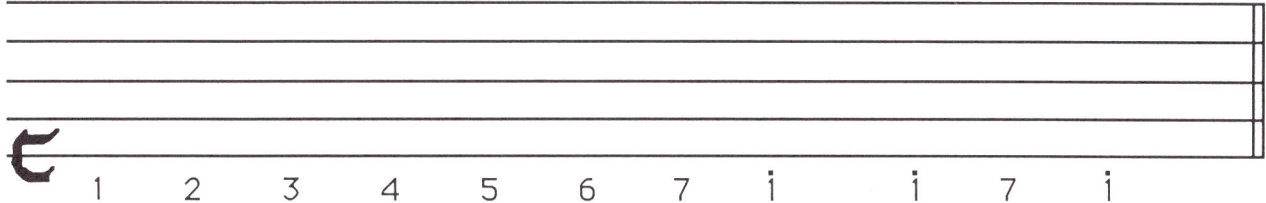

2. From Staff Notation to Number Notation.

Compose a melody of two lines for the rhythm patterns given.

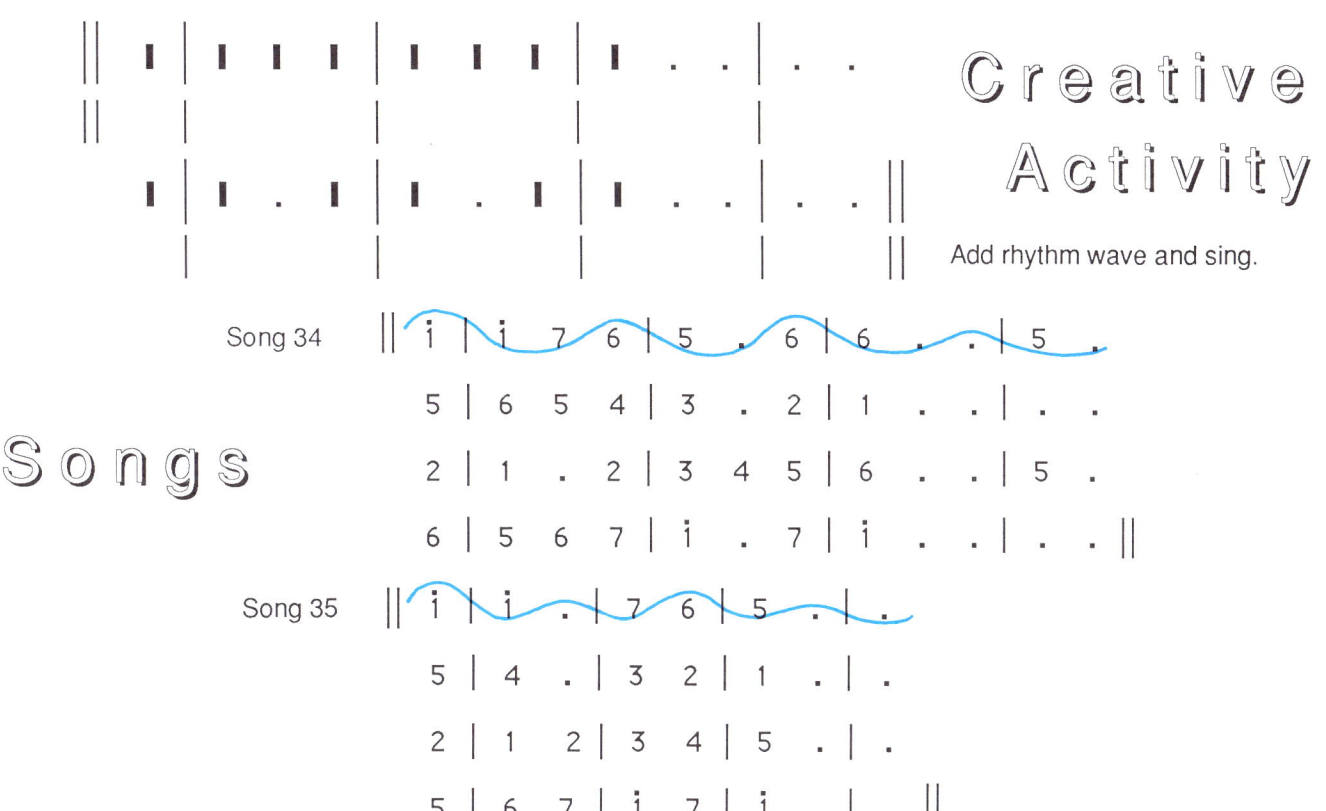

Creative Activity

Add rhythm wave and sing.

Songs

Song 34
```
||  i | i  7  6 | 5  .  6 | 6  .  .  | 5   .
    5 | 6  5  4 | 3  .  2 | 1  .  .  | .   .
    2 | 1  .  2 | 3  4  5 | 6  .  .  | 5   .
    6 | 5  6  7 | i  .  7 | i  .  .  | .   . ||
```

Song 35
```
||  i | i  .  | 7  6 | 5  .  | .
    5 | 4  .  | 3  2 | 1  .  | .
    2 | 1  2  | 3  4 | 5  .  | .
    5 | 6  7  | i  7 | i  .  | .  ||
```

Song 36 - Transcribe to Number Notation. Add rhythm wave.

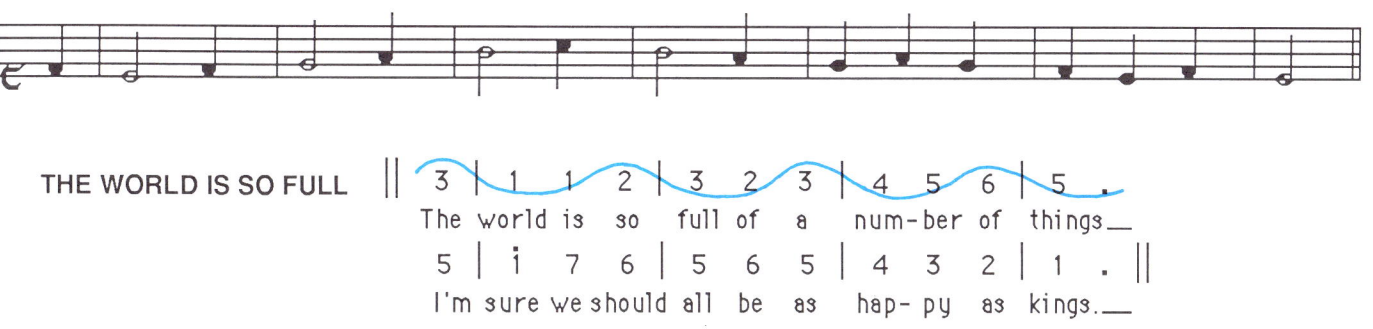

THE WORLD IS SO FULL
```
||  3 | 1  1  2 | 3  2  3 | 4  5  6 | 5  .
   The world is  so  full of  a  num-ber of  things__
    5 | i  7  6 | 5  6  5 | 4  3  2 | 1  . ||
   I'm  sure we should all be  as  hap-py as  kings.__
```

Lesson 15

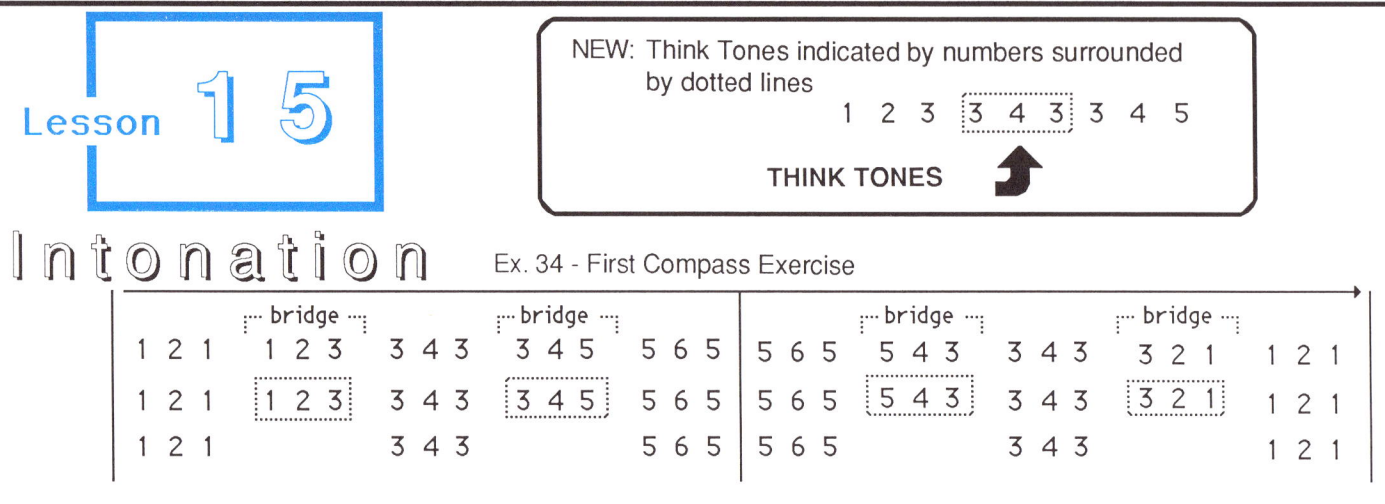

NEW: Think Tones indicated by numbers surrounded by dotted lines

1 2 3 [3 4 3] 3 4 5

THINK TONES

Intonation

Ex. 34 - First Compass Exercise

	bridge			bridge				bridge			bridge		
1 2 1	1 2 3	3 4 3	3 4 5	5 6 5	5 6 5	5 4 3	3 4 3	3 2 1	1 2 1
1 2 1	[1 2 3]	3 4 3	[3 4 5]	5 6 5	5 6 5	[5 4 3]	3 4 3	[3 2 1]	1 2 1
1 2 1		3 4 3		5 6 5	5 6 5		3 4 3		1 2 1

Ear Tests

Rhythm

New Concept: Rhythm phrases that begin on <u>down-pulse</u>.

Rhythm Patterns **Series 7** and Rhythm Gesture IV - Binary

Melodic Application

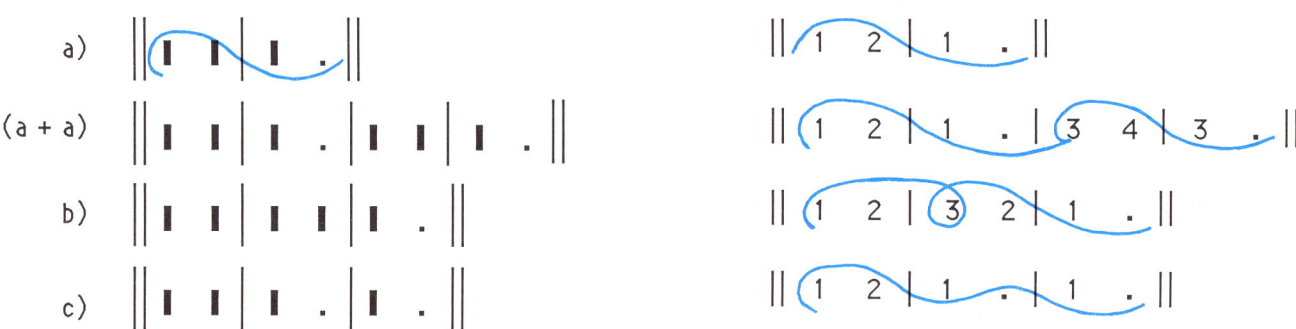

a)

(a + a)

b)

c)

<u>ARSIS - THESIS GESTURE</u> Patterns a) and (a + a)

The *Lift* is called ARSIS and the *landing* is called THESIS.

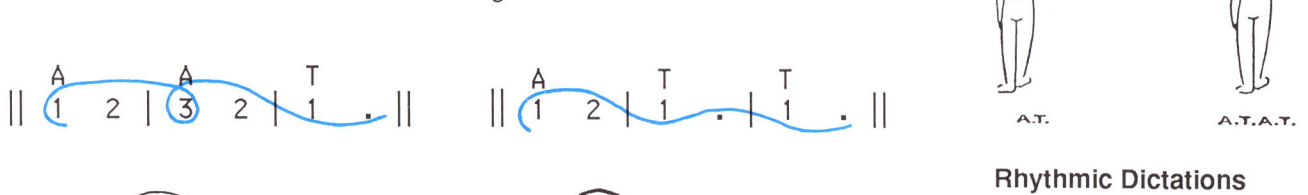

Rhythmic Dictations

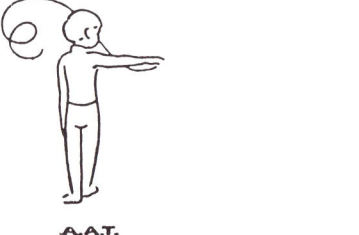

Notation

Transcribe form Number Notation to Staff Notation.

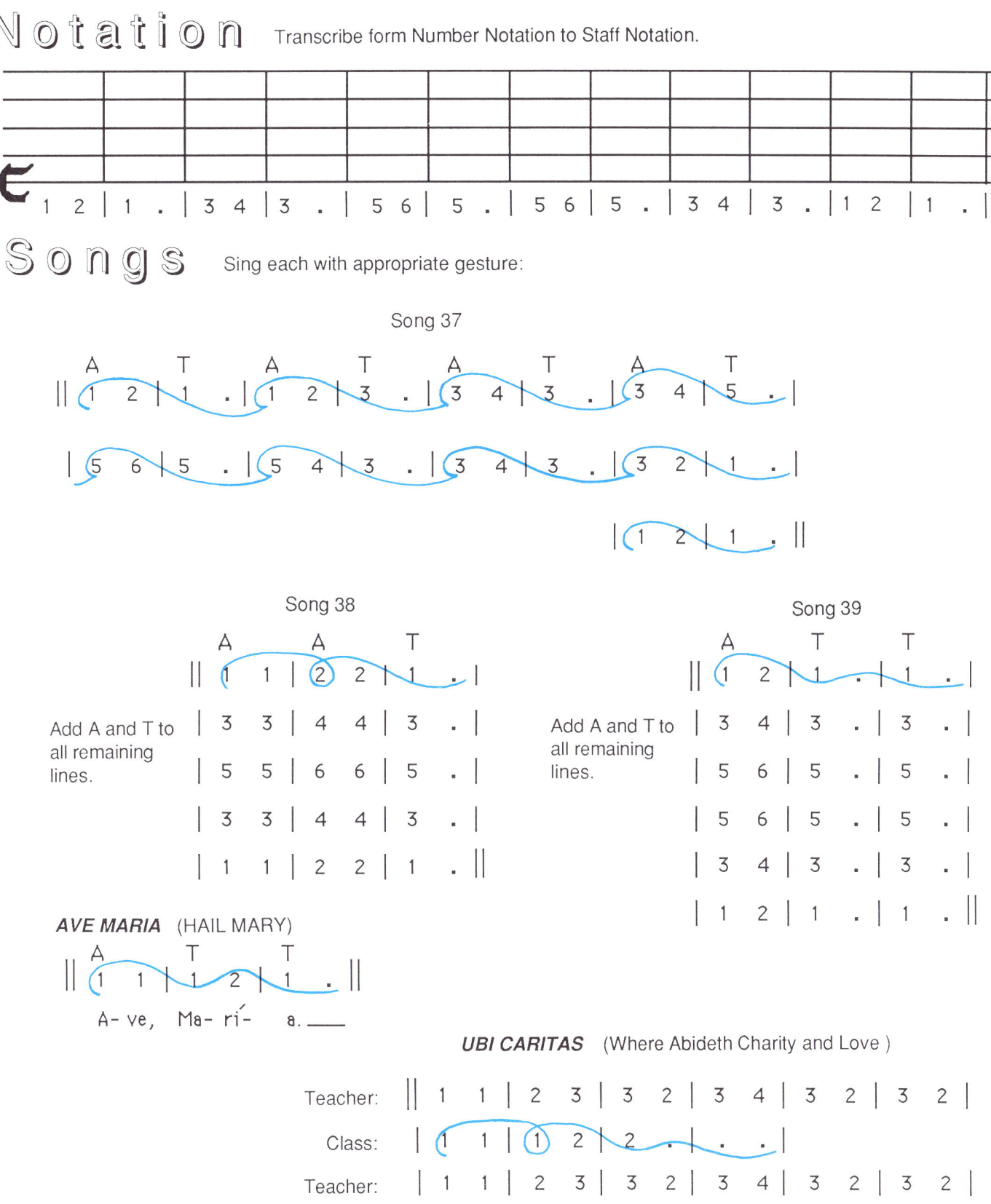

Songs

Sing each with appropriate gesture:

Song 37

| | A | | T | | A | | T | | A | | T | | A | | T | |
| 1 | 2 | 1 | . | 1 | 2 | 3 | . | 3 | 4 | 3 | . | 3 | 4 | 5 | . |

| 5 | 6 | 5 | . | 5 | 4 | 3 | . | 3 | 4 | 3 | . | 3 | 2 | 1 | . |

| 1 | 2 | 1 | . ||

Song 38

| | A | | A | | T | |
| 1 | 1 | 2 | 2 | 1 | . |

Add A and T to all remaining lines.

| 3 | 3 | 4 | 4 | 3 | . |

| 5 | 5 | 6 | 6 | 5 | . |

| 3 | 3 | 4 | 4 | 3 | . |

| 1 | 1 | 2 | 2 | 1 | . ||

AVE MARIA (HAIL MARY)

| | A | | T | | T | |
| 1 | 1 | 1 | 2 | 1 | . ||

A- ve, Ma- ri- a. ____

Song 39

| | A | | T | | T | |
| 1 | 2 | 1 | . | 1 | . |

Add A and T to all remaining lines.

| 3 | 4 | 3 | . | 3 | . |

| 5 | 6 | 5 | . | 5 | . |

| 5 | 6 | 5 | . | 5 | . |

| 3 | 4 | 3 | . | 3 | . |

| 1 | 2 | 1 | . | 1 | . ||

UBI CARITAS (Where Abideth Charity and Love)

Teacher: | 1 1 | 2 3 | 3 2 | 3 4 | 3 2 | 3 2 |

Class: | 1 1 | 1 2 | 2 . | . . |

Teacher: | 1 1 | 2 3 | 3 2 | 3 4 | 3 2 | 3 2 |

Class: | 1 1 | 1 2 | 1 . | . . ||

New Symbol

⸘ = One Pulse Rest

Intonation Exercise 36 First Compass Exercise - Complete Scale

121	123	343	345	565	567i̇	i̇7i̇	i̇7i̇	i̇765	565	543	343	321	121
121	123	343	345	565	567i̇	i̇7i̇	i̇7i̇	i̇765	565	543	343	321	121
121		343		565		i̇7i̇	i̇7i̇		565		343		121

Ear Tests

Rhythm Rhythm Gesture IV - Binary

A.T.A.T.

A.A.T.T.

A.A.A.T.

A.T.T.T

Study with Metrical Language   Melodic Application

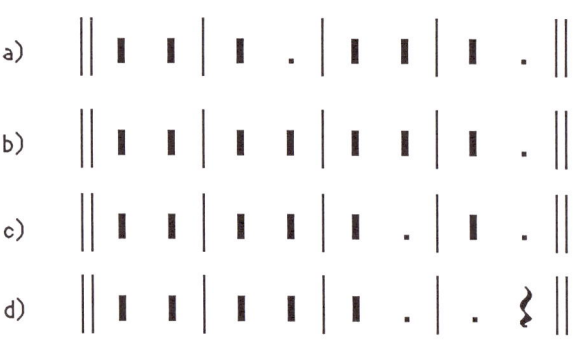

a) ‖ | | | | . | | | | . ‖   ‖ 2 3 | 1 . | 2 3 | 1 . ‖

b) ‖ | | | | | | | | . ‖   ‖ 2 3 | 4 3 | 2 3 | 1 . ‖

c) ‖ | | | | | . | | . ‖   ‖ 1 1 | 1 2 | 3 . | 2 . ‖

d) ‖ | | | | | | . | . ⸘ ‖   ‖ 1 3 | 2 2 | 1 . | . 0 ‖

Rhythmic Dictations

Songs

Song 40

Song 41

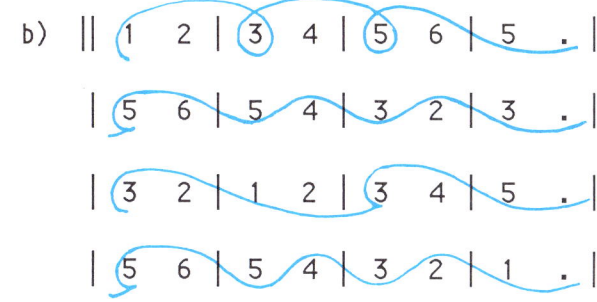

THE FATHER'S LOVE (Beethoven)

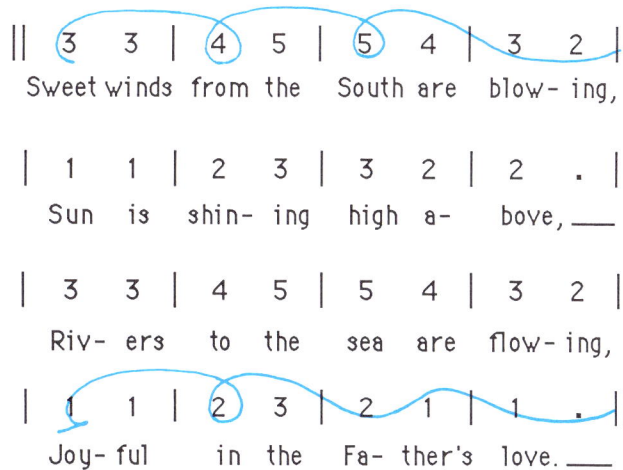

CHURCH BELLS RINGING (French Folk Song)

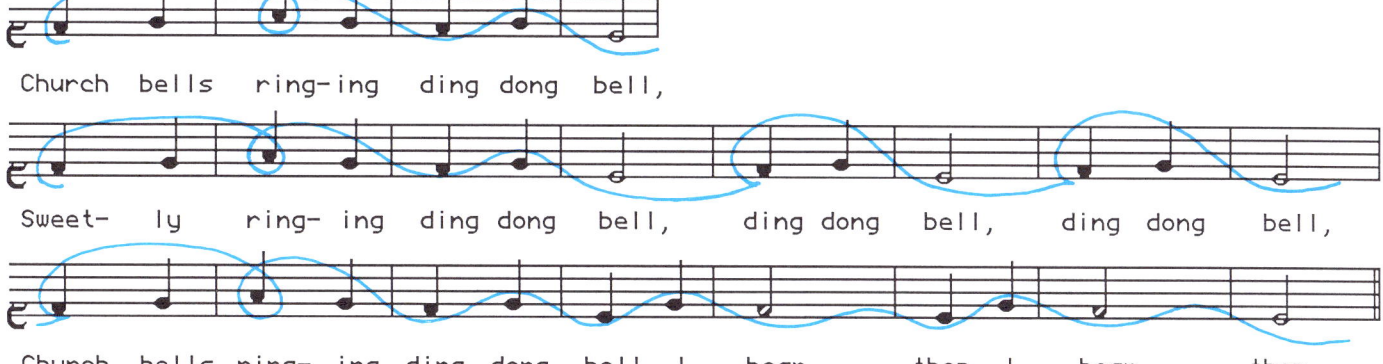

BENEDICAMUS DOMINO (Let Us Bless the Lord. Thanks be to God.)

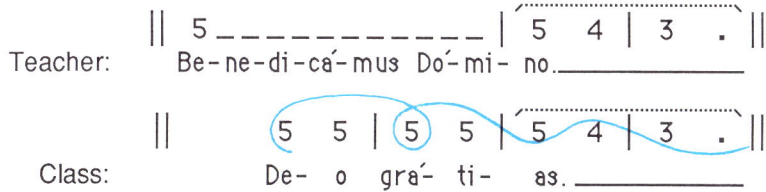

Lesson **17**

Intonation

Exercise 37   -   First Compass Exercise

1 2 1	3 4 3	5 6 5	1̇ 7 1̇	1̇ 7 1̇	5 6 5	3 4 3	1 2 1
1 2 1	3 4 3	5 6 5	1̇ 7 1̇	1̇ 7 1̇	5 6 5	3 4 3	1 2 1
1 2 1	3 4 3	5 6 5	1̇ 7 1̇	1̇ 7 1̇	5 6 5	3 4 3	1 2 1
1 2 1	3 4 3	5 6 5	1̇ 7 1̇	1̇ 7 1̇	5 6 5	3 4 3	1 2 1

Exercise 38   -   Second Compass Exercise

Ear Tests

121	343	565	1̇71̇	1̇71̇	565	343	121
121	343	565	1̇71̇	1̇71̇	565	343	121
1	3	5	1̇	1̇	5	3	1

Rhythm

Compose a melody for each rhythm given.

e) ‖ ▮ . | ▮ ▮ | ▮ ▮ | ▮ . ‖ ⟶

f) ‖ ▮ . | ▮ ▮ | ▮ . | ▮ . ‖ ⟶

g) ‖ ▮ . | ▮ ▮ | ▮ . | . . ‖ ⟶

Rhythmic Dictations

Notation
Transcribe to Staff Notation and sing.

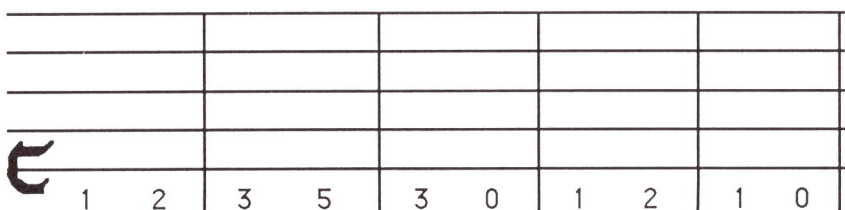

| | 1 2 | 3 5 | 3 0 | 1 2 | 1 0 |

Songs

GOOSEY, GOOSEY, GANDER

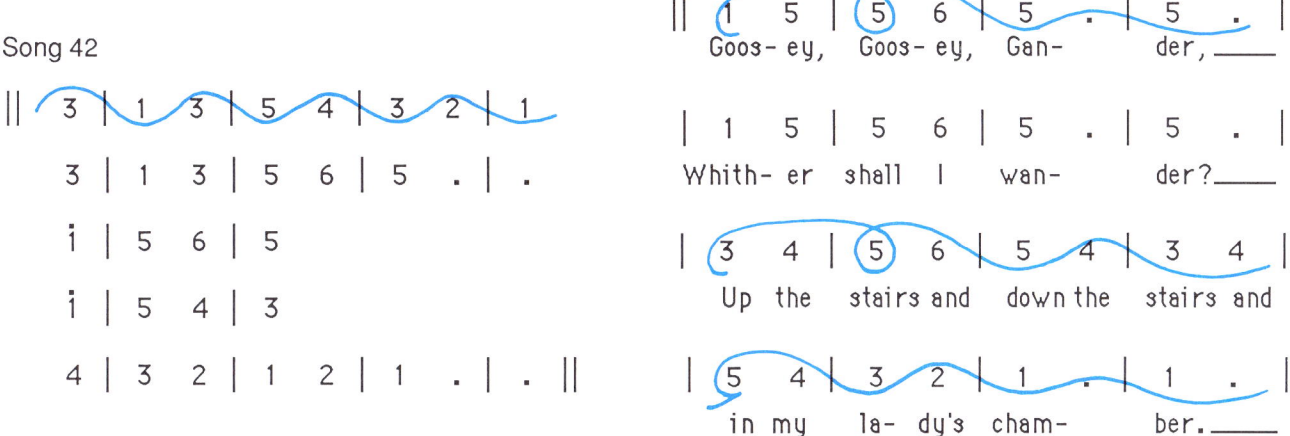

Song 42

Song 43 *Basque Melody*

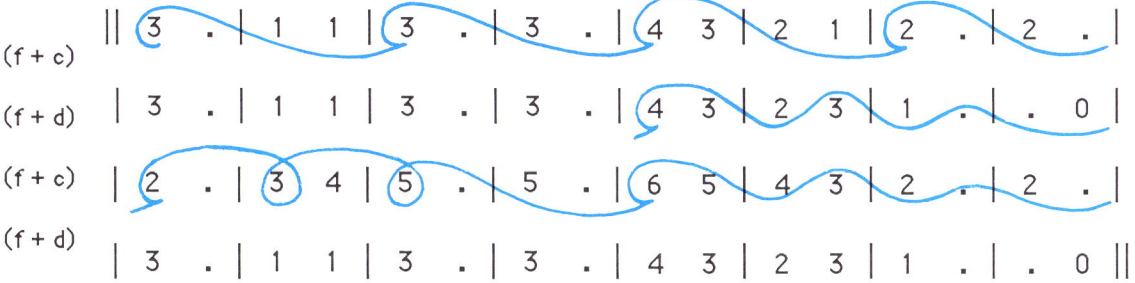

HARK, HARK, THE DOGS DO BARK

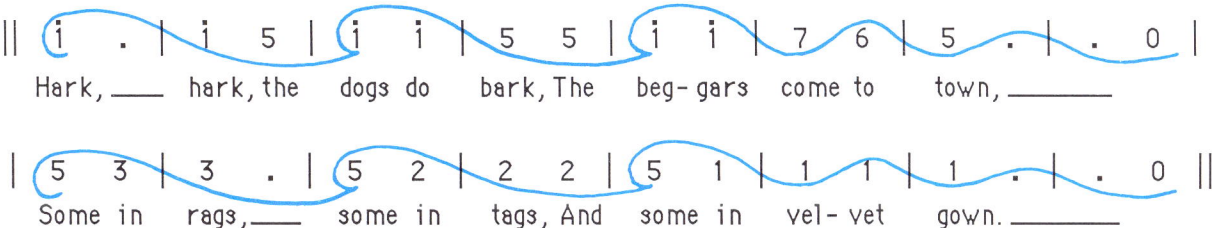

Lesson **18**

Intonation

Exercise 39

```
a)                    b)
| 1  3  5    5  3  1  | 5  3  1    1  3  5 →
| 1  3  5   [5] 3  1  | 5  3  1   [1] 3  5
| 1  3  5       3  1  | 5  3  1       3  5
```

Exercise 40

```
a)                      b)
| 1  3  5  3  1   | 5  3  1  3  5 →
| 1  3  5  3  5   | 5  3  1  3  1
| 1  3  3  5  3   | 5  3  3  1  3
| 1  3  5  5  3   | 5  3  1  1  3
| 1  3  1  3  5   | 5  3  5  3  1
```

Ear Tests

Exercise 41

```
| 1  3  5    5  1̇  | 1̇  5  5  3  1   →
| 1  3  5    1̇  5  | 1̇  5  5  3  5
| 1  3  5    1̇  5  1̇ | 1̇  5  3  5  3  1
```

Rhythm   Rhythm Gesture IV - Ternary

Rhythm Patterns - **Series 9**   Practice single lines and in combination with other lines
                                   as was done in previous chapters.

Melodic Application

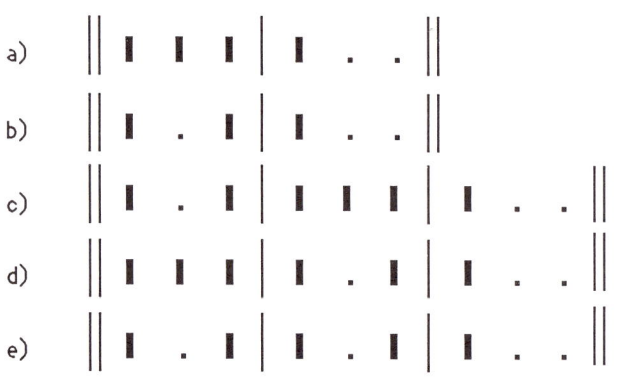

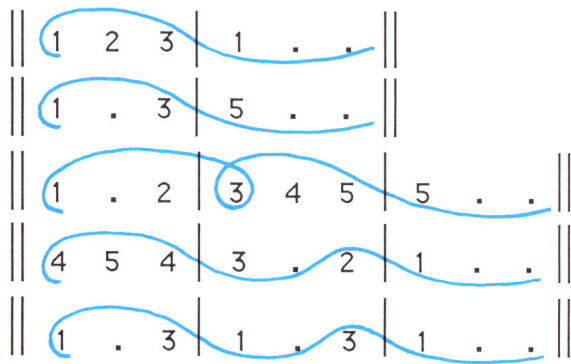

Rhythmic Dictations

Songs

Song 46   ‖ 1 . 2 | 3 . . |

| 3 . 4 | 3 . 2 | 3 . . |

| 1 . 2 | 3 . . |

| 3 . 4 | 3 . 2 | 1 . . ‖

Song 47   Review Rhythm Gesture III
             Transcribe to Number Notation   *French Folk Melody*

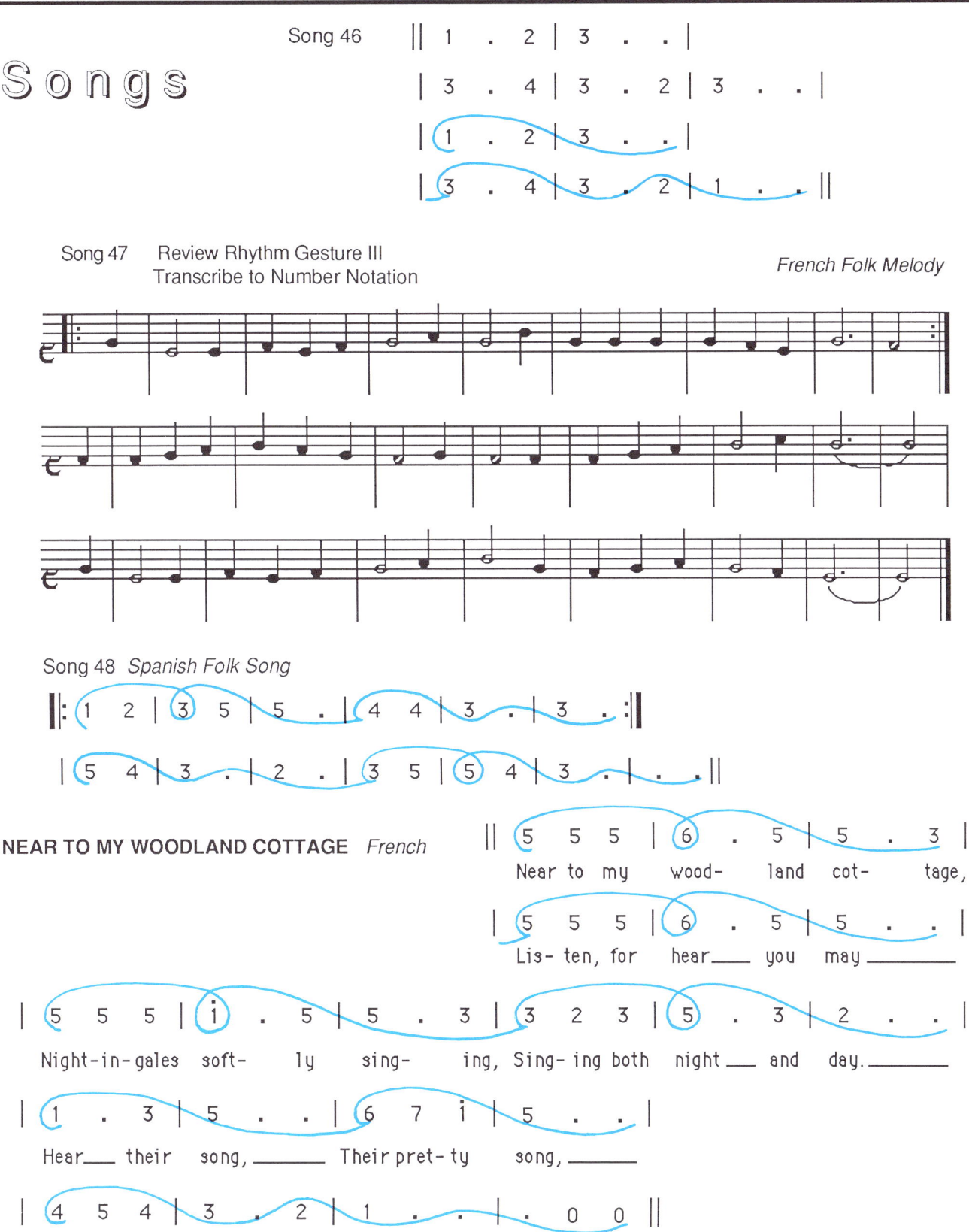

Song 48 *Spanish Folk Song*

‖: 1 2 3 5 | 5 . | 4 4 | 3 . | 3 . :‖

| 5 4 | 3 . | 2 . | 3 5 | 5 4 | 3 . | . . ‖

NEAR TO MY WOODLAND COTTAGE *French*   ‖ 5 5 5 | 6 . 5 | 5 . 3 |
                                                  Near to my   wood- land cot-   tage,

| 5 5 5 | 6 . 5 | 5 . . |
Lis- ten, for hear___ you may _____

| 5 5 5 | 1 . 5 | 5 . 3 | 3 2 3 | 5 . 3 | 2 . . |
Night-in-gales soft- ly sing- ing, Sing-ing both night___ and day. _____

| 1 . 3 | 5 . . | 6 7 1 | 5 . . |
Hear___ their song, _____ Their pret-ty   song, _____

| 4 5 4 | 3 . 2 | 1 . . | . 0 0 ‖
In the sweet month ___ of May. _____

Lesson 19

Intonation

Exercise 42

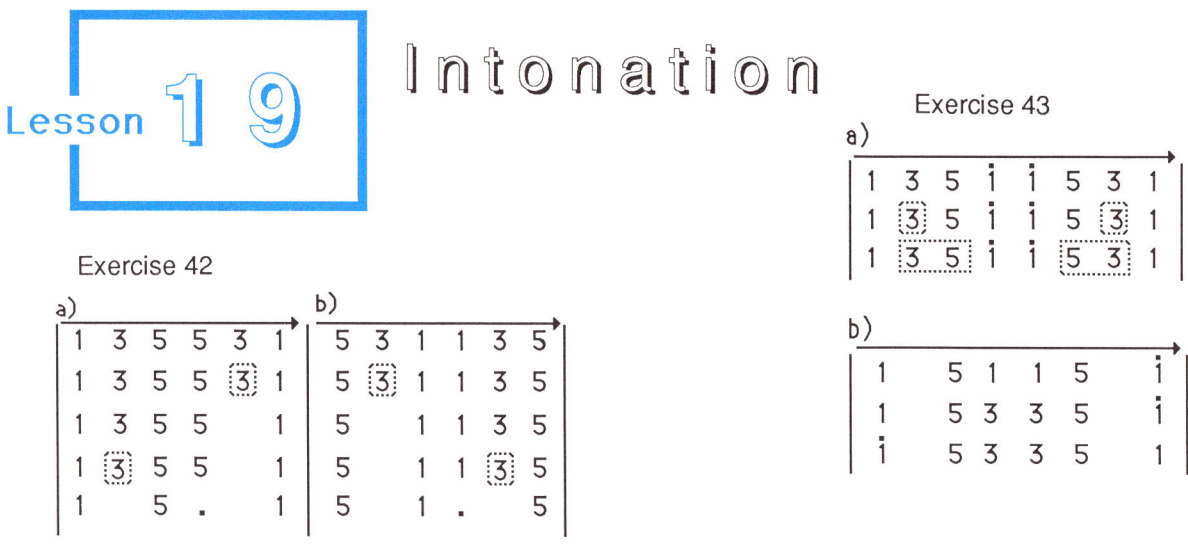

Ear Tests

Rhythm

Compose a melody for each rhythm given. Add chironomy and sing.

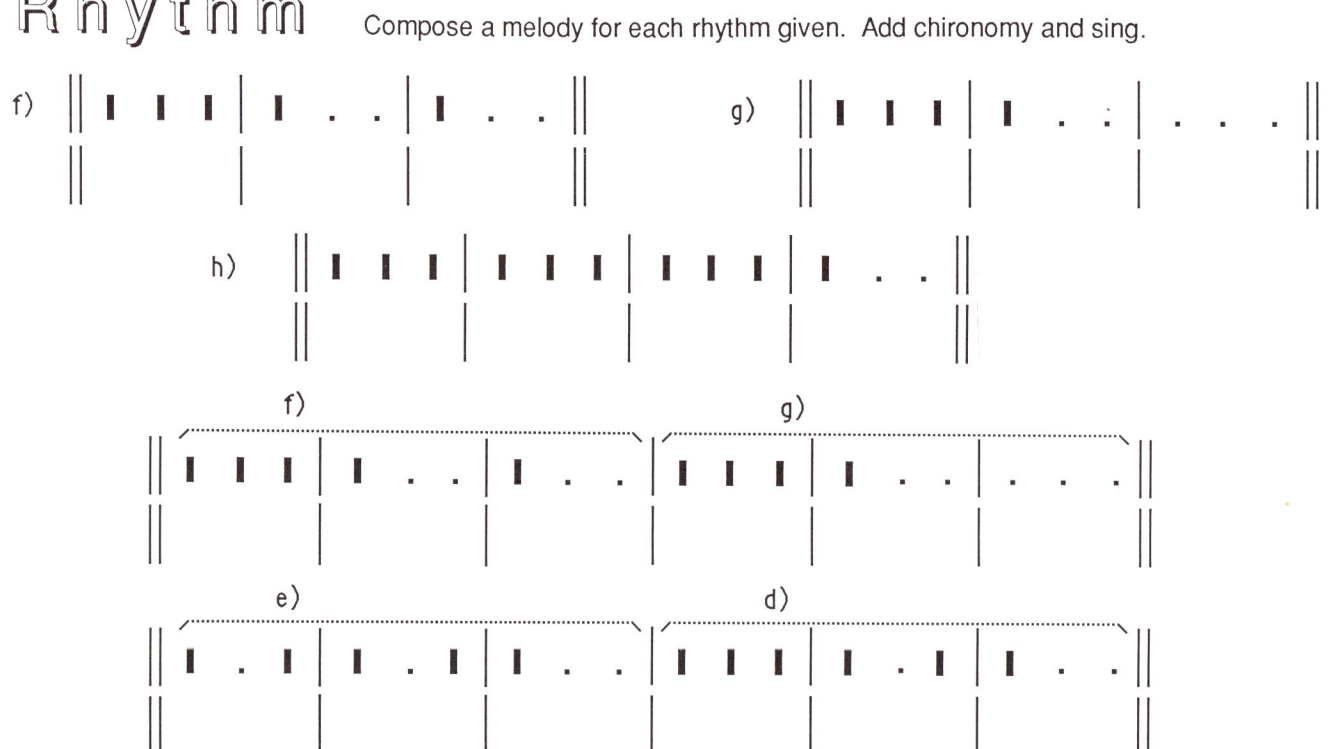

Rhythmic Dictations

Songs

Song 49   Transcribe to Staff Notation and sing.

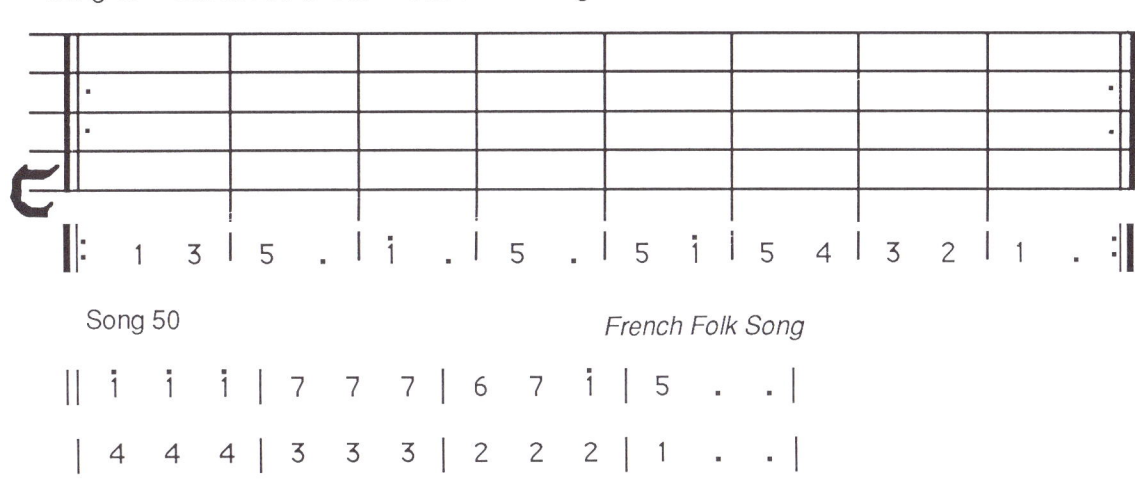

Song 50   *French Folk Song*

|| i̇ i̇ i̇ | 7 7 7 | 6 7 i̇ | 5 . . |

| 4 4 4 | 3 3 3 | 2 2 2 | 1 . . |

| 1 2 3 | 1 2 3 | 1 2 3 | 4 . . |

| 2 3 4 | 2 3 4 | 2 3 4 | 5 . . |

| i̇ 7 6 | 5 4 3 | 2 1 2 | 1 . . ||

German Folk Song

Song 51   Transcribe to Number Notation and sing.

FOR THE GIFT OF DAILY BREAD   *German Folk Song*

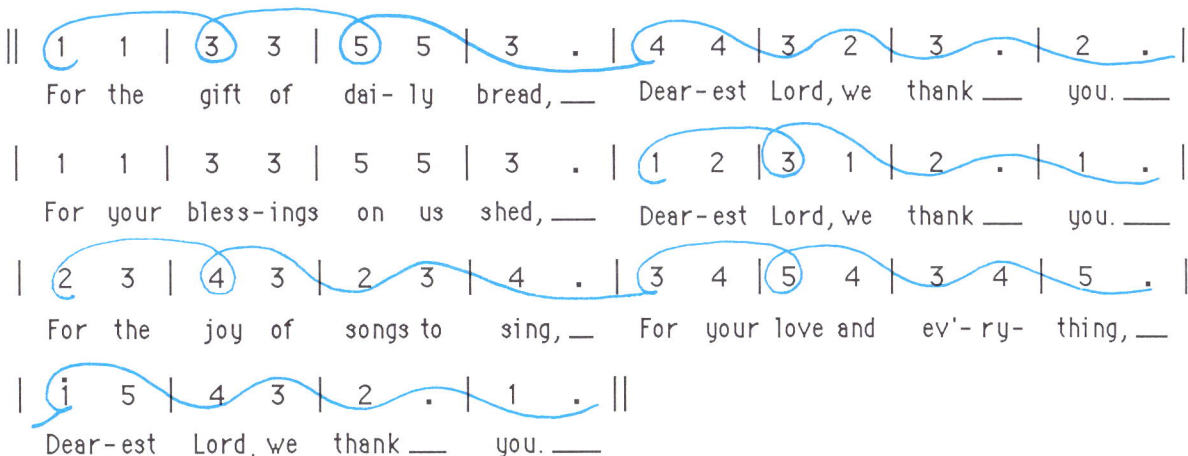

Intonation

Exercise 44   -   Third Compass Exercise

```
| 1 2 1   3 4 3   5 6 5   i 7 i | i 7 i   5 6 5   3 4 3   1 2 1 |
| 1 2 1   3 4 3   5 6 5   i 7 i | i 7 i   5 6 5   3 4 3   1 2 1 |
|   2 1     4 3     6 5     7 i |   7 i     6 5     4 3     2 1 |
```

Ear Tests

Rhythm

Rhythm Gesture IV - Binary (Review)

a) ‖ ▮ ▮ | ▮ . ‖   ‖ 1   2 | 1   . ‖

(a + a) ‖ ▮ ▮ | ▮ . | ▮ ▮ | ▮ . ‖   ‖ 1   3 | 5   . | 5   6 | 5   . ‖

b) ‖ ▮ ▮ | ▮ ▮ | ▮ . ‖   ‖ 1   1 | 5   6 | 5   . ‖

c) ‖ ▮ ▮ | ▮ . | ▮ . ‖   ‖ 5   4 | 3   . | 3   . ‖

Creative Activity

Combine patterns and compose a melody for each:

(a + b)

(b + a)

Rhythmic Dictations

Songs

TWINKLE, TWINKLE, LITTLE STAR

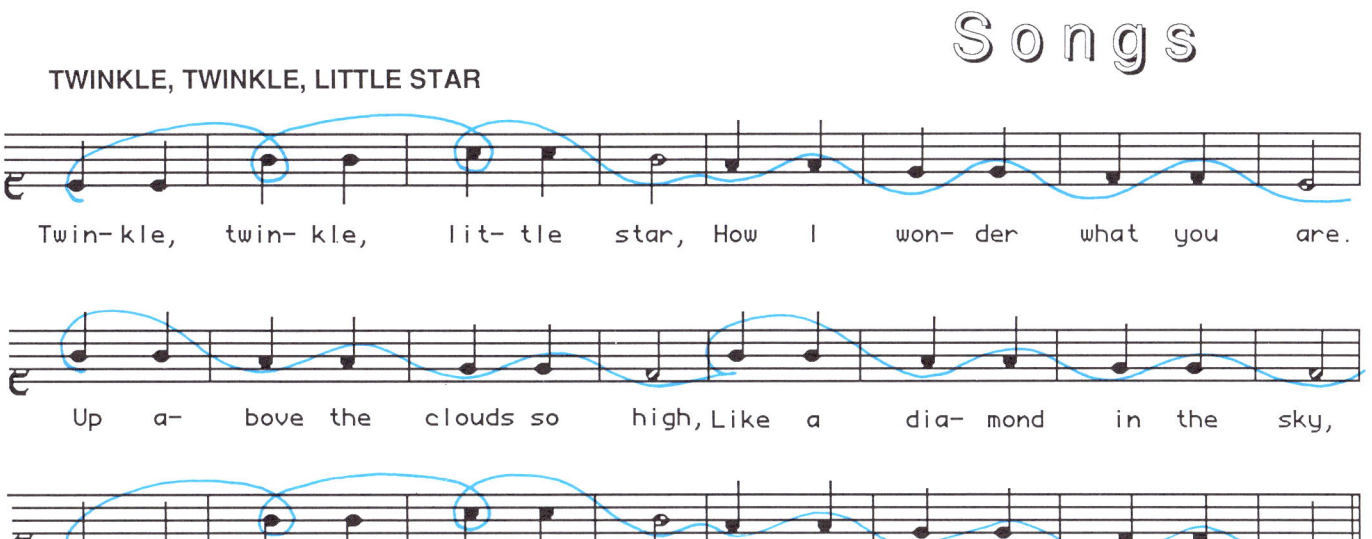

Twin-kle, twin-kle, lit-tle star, How I won-der what you are.

Up a- bove the clouds so high, Like a dia-mond in the sky,

Twin-kle, twin-kle, lit-tle star, How I won-der what you are.

Song 52   Transcribe to Staff Notation:

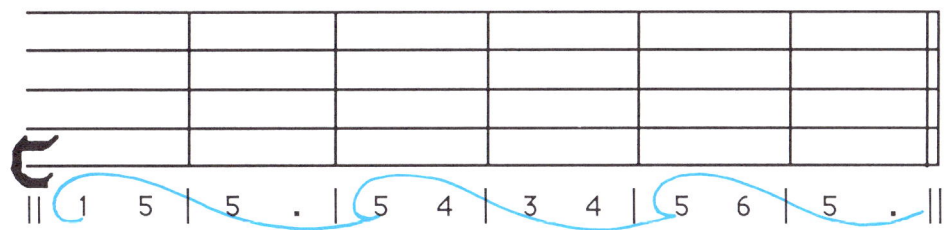

|| 1 5 | 5 . | 5 4 | 3 4 | 5 6 | 5 . ||

WHERE ABIDETH CHARITY AND LOVE   *Gregorian Chant*

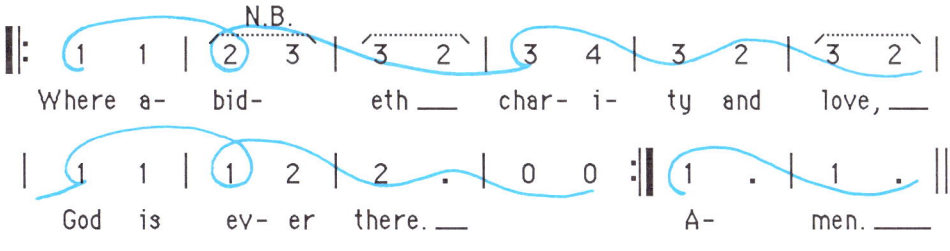

N.B.

||: 1 1 | 2 3 | 3 2 | 3 4 | 3 2 | 3 2 |
Where a- bid- eth __ char-i- ty and love, __

| 1 1 | 1 2 | 2 . | 0 0 :|| 1 . | 1 . ||
God is ev- er there. __   A- men. __

N.B. Note Slur: Sing
Two notes for each
syllable

HOW DO YOU LIKE TO GO UP IN A SWING?

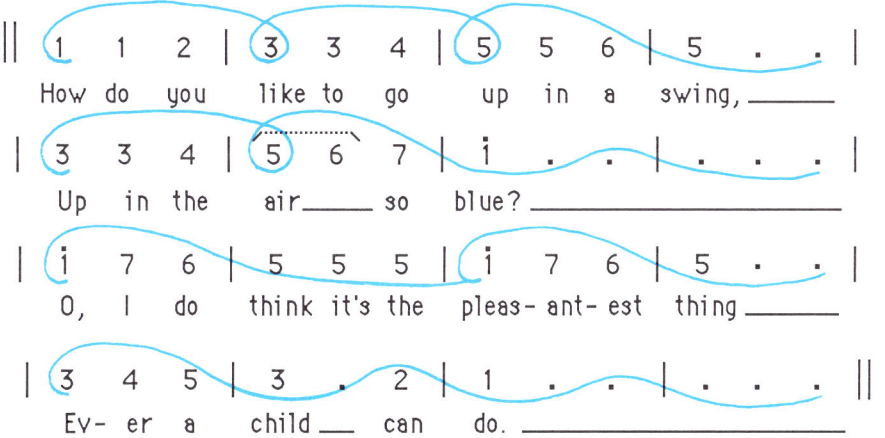

|| 1 1 2 | 3 3 4 | 5 5 6 | 5 . . |
How do you like to go up in a swing, ____

| 3 3 4 | 5 6 7 | i̇ . . | . . . |
Up in the air ___ so blue? ____

| i̇ 7 6 | 5 5 5 | i̇ 7 6 | 5 . . |
O, I do think it's the pleas-ant-est thing ____

| 3 4 5 | 3 . 2 | 1 . . | . . . ||
Ev- er a child ___ can do. ____

Robert L. Stevenson

Lesson 21

Intonation

Exercise 45

1	2	3	1	2		1		3	4			3
1	3	5	1	3	4		3			5	6	5
1	3	5	1				3			6	5	

5	3	5	5	4	3		5	6	5
5	3	5	5		3		5	6	5

3	1	5	3	2	1		5	6	5
3	1	5	3		1		5	6	5
3	5	1	3	5	6		5	3	2	1

Exercise 46 - Fourth Compass Exercise

1	2	1	2	1	4	3	6	5		6	5	4	3	2	1	1	2	1
1	2	1	2	1	4	3	6	5		6	5	4	3	2	1	1	2	1
1	2	1	2		4		6			6		4		2		1	2	1

Memorize last line

Ear Tests

Creative Activity   Compose a melody for each rhythm given:

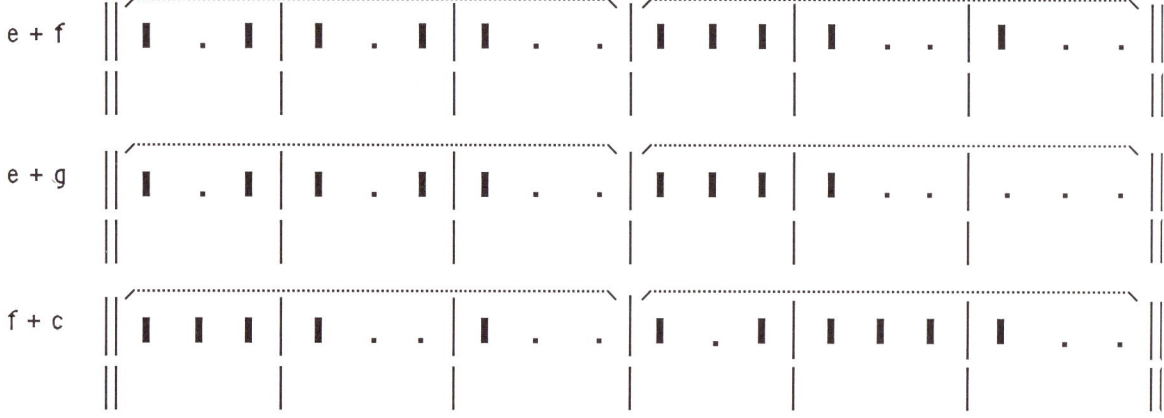

Rhythmic Dictations

Song 53

Songs

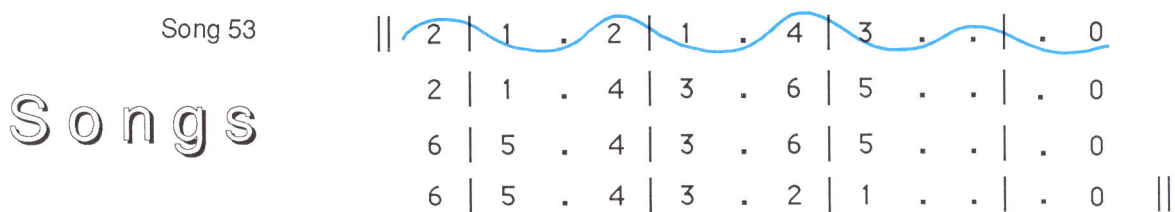

```
|| 2 | 1 . 2 | 1 . 4 | 3 . . | . 0
   2 | 1 . 4 | 3 . 6 | 5 . . | . 0
   6 | 5 . 4 | 3 . 6 | 5 . . | . 0
   6 | 5 . 4 | 3 . 2 | 1 . . | . 0 ||
```

NOW THAT DAYLIGHT FILLS THE SKY

Gregorian Chant

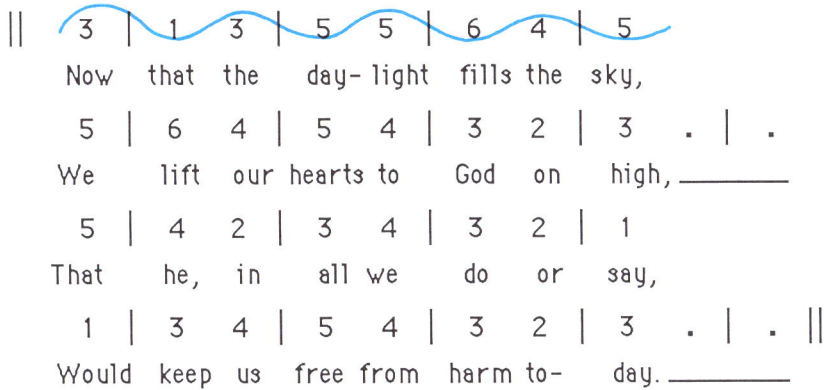

```
|| 3 | 1  3 | 5  5 | 6  4 | 5
   Now  that the day-light fills the sky,

   5 | 6  4 | 5  4 | 3  2 | 3 . | .
   We  lift our hearts to God on high,_____

   5 | 4  2 | 3  4 | 3  2 | 1
   That he, in all we do or say,

   1 | 3  4 | 5  4 | 3  2 | 3 . | . ||
   Would keep us free from harm to- day._____
```

BEHOLD THE RISING OF THE MOON

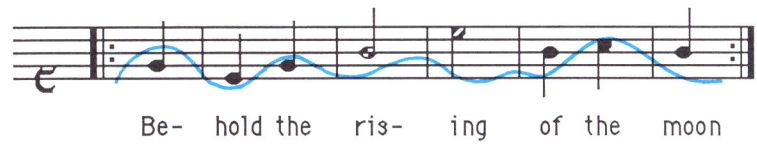

Be- hold the ris- ing of the moon

That shin-eth in the month of June, That shin-eth in the month of June.

|1.| |2.|

Ris- ing moon, shin-ing moon, Ris- ing in the month of June. June._____

Song 54   **SANTA CATALINA**

Spanish Folk Song

Transcribe to Number Notation

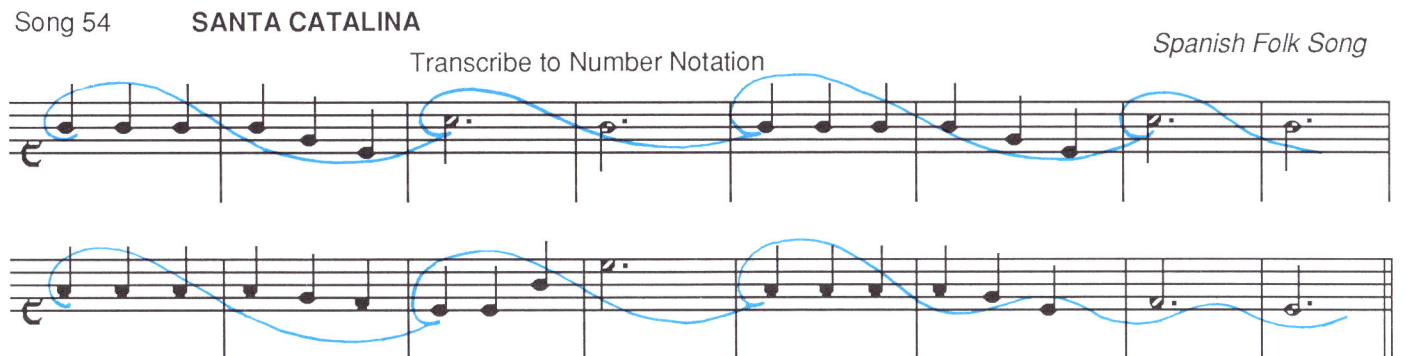

Intonation

Exercise 47

a)   b)

1	2	3		4	2	1
1		3		4	2	1
1		3		2	4	3
3		1		2	4	3

3	4	5		4	2	3
3		5		4	2	3
5		3		4	2	3
5		3		2	4	3

Ear Tests

Exercise 48

1	3	5		6	5	4	3
1	3	5		6		4	3
1	3	5		4	5	6	5
1	3	5		4	6	5	4	3
1	3	5		6	4	5	6	5

Rhythm

Aural Training in Rhythm

Dictations without melody

Dictations with melody

Songs

*American Folk Song from
the Appalachian Mountains*

GO AND TELL AUNT NANCY

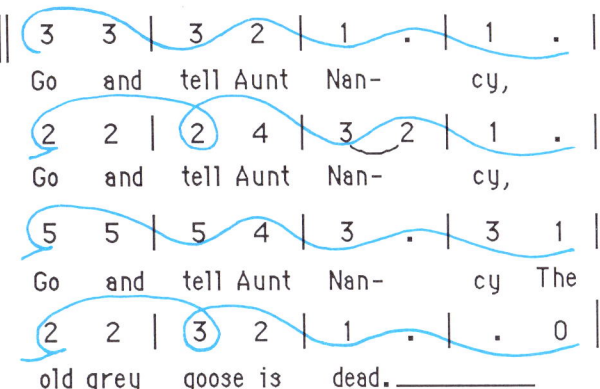

```
|| 3  3 | 3  2 | 1  .  | 1  .  |
   Go and  tell Aunt Nan-    cy,

   2  2 | 2  4 | 3  2 | 1  .  |
   Go and  tell Aunt Nan-    cy,

   5  5 | 5  4 | 3  .  | 3  1 |
   Go and  tell Aunt Nan-  cy  The

   2  2 | 3  2 | 1  .  | .  0 ||
   old grey  goose is  dead._____
```

O HOLY SPIRIT, LORD OF GRACE

```
|| 1 | 3  4 | 5  5 | 6  6 | 5
   O   Ho- ly  Spi- rit,  Lord of Grace,

   5 | 1  7 | 6  6 | 5  .  | .
   E- ter- nal  source of  love,_____

   1 | 3  4 | 5  5 | 6  6 | 5
   In- flame, we  pray,  our  in-most  heart,

   1 | 4  3 | 2  2 | 1  .  | .  ||
   With  fire from heav'n a-  bove._____
```

Transcribe to
Staff Notation

O COCK-A-DOODLE DOO!

English Folk Song

```
|| 1 | 1  3 | 3  2 | 3  .  | .  3 | 1  3 | 3  2 | 3  .  | .
   O   cock-a- doo- dle  doo!_____  My   dame has  lost her  shoe!_____

   5 | 1  1 | 7  6 | 5  3 | 1  2 | 3  5 | 3  2 | 1  .  | .
   My  mas- ter's lost his  fid-dling stick, They  don't know what  to   do,_____

   1 | 1  3 | 3  2 | 3  .  | .  3 | 5  6 | 5  3 | 5  .  | .
   They  don't know what  to   do._____  They  don't know what  to   do;_____

   5 | 1  1 | 7  6 | 5  3 | 1  2 | 3  5 | 3  2 | 1  .  | .  ||
   My  mas- ter's lost his  fid-dling stick, They  don't know what  to   do._____
```

Intonation

Exercise 49

```
| 1  3  5  6  4  3              ⟶
| 1  3  5  6  4  5
| 1  3  5  6  4  2           1
| 1  3  5  6  4  5  [3] 2  1 |
```

Exercise 50

```
| 5  i  5    5  6  7  i  6  5   ⟶
| 5  i  5    5  6     i  6  5
| 5  i  5    6 [5]4 [3] 6  5
| 5  i  5    4 [3 5] 6 [5] 4 [3] 5 |
```

Ear Tests

Rhythm

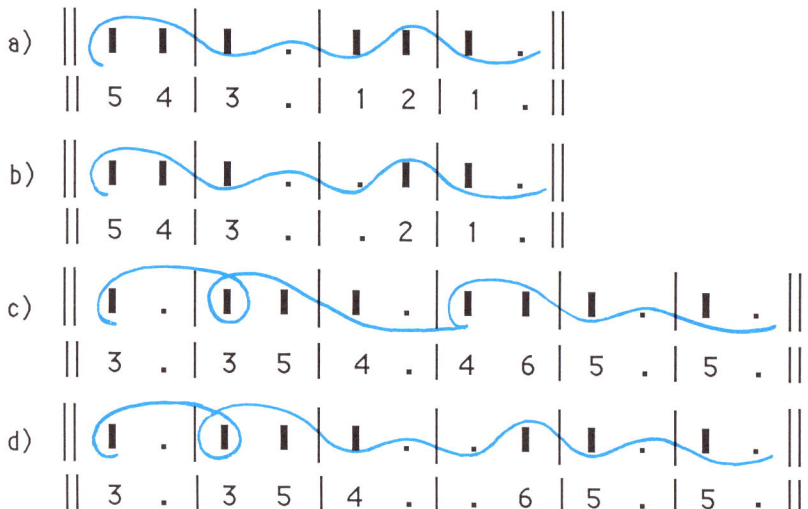

a)
```
|| 5  4 | 3  . | 1  2 | 1  . ||
```

b)
```
|| 5  4 | 3  . | .  2 | 1  . ||
```

c)
```
|| 3  . | 3  5 | 4  . | 4  6 | 5  . | 5  . ||
```

d)
```
|| 3  . | 3  5 | 4  . | .  6 | 5  . | 5  . ||
```

Rhythmic Dictations

Song 55   *Spanish Lullabye*

REGINA CAELI   (Queen of Heaven)

Group I || 1 2 | 1 2 | 3 . | 4 3 | 2 .
           Re- gí- na cáe- li,_____ lae- tá- re

Group II   4 | 3 2 | 1 . ||
           al- le- lú- ia._____

S o n g s

Song 56 || 5 5 | i i | 5 5 | 6 . | 5 5 | i i | 6 6 | 5 . |
           | 5 5 | i i | 5 5 | 6 . | 5 4 | 3 2 | 1 . | 1 . |

Basque Melody
           | 3 . | 3 . | 4 . | 6 . | 5 4 | 3 2 | 3 . | 1 . |
           | 3 . | 3 . | 4 . | 6 . | 5 4 | 3 2 | 1 . | . . ||

Song 57 || 3 . | 3 5 | 4 . | . 6 | 5 . | 5 . |
           | 3 . | 3 5 | 4 . | . 6 | 5 . | . . |

Catalan Melody
           | 3 . | 3 5 | 4 . | . 2 | 1 . | 2 . |
           | 3 . | 3 5 | 4 . | . 2 | 1 . | . . ||

CHILDREN OF YOUR HEAV'NLY KING || 1 . 1 | 5 . 3 | 4 5 6 | 5 . . |
                                       Chil- dren of____ your heav'n- ly King,_____

| 1 . 1 | 5 . 3 | 4 5 6 | 5 . . |
As____ you jour- ney, sweet- ly sing;_____

| 5 . 5 | i 7 6 | 5 . 4 | 3 . . |
Sing____ your Sa- vior's worth- y praise,_____

| 4 5 6 | 5 . 3 | 2 1 2 | 1 . . ||
Glo- rious in his works____ and ways,_____

John Cennick, 1742

From Chapter 3   **THE FLOWERS AWAKE**   A "Conversation Song"

| | | | | | | | | | |
|1|1|1|1|1|1|1|1|1|2|

TEACHER: A   cro-cus   lifts her   love-ly   head to   say:

|1|2|2|1|.|.|
CHILDREN: Al-   le-   lu-   ia! _____

|2|3|3|3|3|3|3|2|1|2|
TEACHER: A   gold-en   daf-fo-   dil be-   gins to   pray:

|1|2|2|1|.|.|
CHILDREN: Al-   le-   lu-   ia! _____

|2|3|4|5|4|3|4|5|
TEACHER: Out   of   the earth with   song-ful   mirth,

|5|5|4|3|3|2|1|2|
The   flow-ers spring. I   hear them   sing:

|1|2|2|2|1|2|1|.|.|
CHILDREN: Al-   le-   lu-   ia! A-   men. _____

From Chapter 11   **REJOICE, REJOICE, O ISRAEL**

|6|6|6|6|6|6|6|5|.|.|
I –   Re-   joice, re-   joice, O   Is-ra-   el, _____

|6|6|6|6|6|6|6|5|.|.|
II –   Thy   Sa-vior comes, Em-   man-u-   el, _____

|5|5|4|3|.|3|.|.|
I & II –   Al-   le-   lu-   ia. _____

From Chapter 12   **A CHILD IS BORN IN BETHLEHEM**

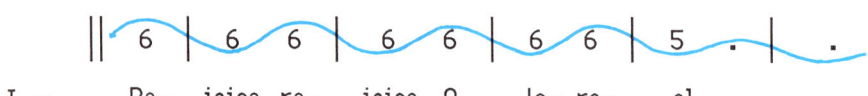

|1|1|1|1|1|1|1|1|1|2|3|1|.|.|

1 A   child is   born in   Beth-le-   hem, al-   le-lu-   ia! _____
2. O   come, a-   dore as   An-gels   sing, al-   le-lu-   ia! _____
3. Then   sing we   high, then   sing we   low: al-   le-lu-   ia! _____

|3|3|3|3|3|3|3|3|

1. Glad   ti-dings   for Je-   ru-sa-   lem,
2. And   give our hearts to   Christ, our   King,
3. Be-   ne-di-   ca-mus   Do-mi-   no.

|3|2|1|2|3|2|.|.|1|2|3|1|.|.|

1.-3.   al-   le-   lu-   ia, _____   al-   le-lu-   ia. _____